MARY, MOTHER OF GOD

MARY, MOTHER OF GOD

Edited by

Carl E. Braaten and Robert W. Jenson

WILLIAM B. EERDMANS PUBLISHING COMPANY
GRAND RAPIDS, MICHIGAN / CAMBRIDGE, U.K.

Wm. B. Eerdmans Publishing Co.
255 Jefferson Ave. S.E., Grand Rapids, Michigan 49503 /
P.O. Box 163, Cambridge CB3 9PU U.K.

Printed in the United States of America

09 08 07 06 05 04   7 6 5 4 3 2 1

Library of Congress Cataloging-in-Publication Data

Mary, Mother of God / edited by Carl E. Braaten and Robert W. Jenson.
        p.   cm.
Originally addresses given at a conference held
June 9-11, 2002 at St. Olaf College, Northfield, Minn.
Includes bibliographical references.
ISBN 0-8028-2266-5 (pbk.: alk. paper)
1. Mary, Blessed Virgin, Saint — Congresses.
I. Braaten, Carl E., 1929-   II. Jenson, Robert W.

BT595.M345   2004
32.91 — dc22

                                        2004043417

www.eerdmans.com

Contents

Preface

Since the Council of Ephesus, A.D. 431, orthodox Christianity has confessed that Mary is the "Mother of God." Admittedly, Mary is never called "Mother of God" in the New Testament and the title was hotly contested in the Christological controversies of the fifth century. But the title "Mother of God" seemed inevitable once the confession that Jesus is truly God — "of one substance with the Father" — was placed at the center of the faith defined at Nicaea.

Mary's title as Mother of God has not fared well in Protestant Christianity. The vehement attack of the Reformation against the exaggerated cult of Mary in late-medieval Christianity diminished her place in the story of salvation, personal piety, and public worship. This occurred despite Luther's high view of Mary. His Christmas meditations, exposition of the Magnificat[1] and of the Hail Mary[2] extol the Virgin who, faced with the role of bearing the Messiah, lived by faith alone. Luther wrote: "Men have crowded all her glory into a single word, calling her the Mother of God. . . . It needs to be pondered in the heart what it means to be the Mother of God. . . . In order to become the Mother of God, she had to be a woman, a virgin, of the tribe of Judah, and had to believe the angelic

---

1. *Luther's Works,* vol. 21, ed. Jaroslav Pelikan (Saint Louis: Concordia, 1956), pp. 297-355.

2. *Luther's Works,* vol. 43, ed. Gustav K. Wiencke (Philadelphia: Fortress, 1968), pp. 39-41.

message in order to become worthy as the Scriptures foretold. . . . Mary does not desire to be an idol; she does nothing, God does all. We ought to call upon her, that for her sake God may grant and do what we request. Thus also all other saints are to be invoked, so that the work may be every way God's alone."[3]

Luther taught that in the proper use of the words of the Hail Mary we are not only giving praise and honor to Mary but also giving God all the glory for what he has accomplished through her. He said: "Laud and love her simply as the one who, without merit, obtained such blessings from God, sheerly out of his mercy, as she herself testifies in the Magnificat (Luke 1:46-55)."[4]

Virtually all that was retained in the Protestant tradition of Luther's Marian devotion was his harsh criticisms of the abuses. Renewed interest in a theology of Mary was sparked in modern times by the Second Vatican Council and the ensuing ecumenical dialogues.[5] The Council made clear that Mary is firmly connected to Christ and the church, and does not play an independent role in the mediation of salvation.

The essays in this volume were originally given as addresses at a theological conference on "Mary, Mother of God," sponsored by the Center for Catholic and Evangelical Theology, at St. Olaf College, Northfield, Minnesota, June 9-11, 2002. The conference brought scholars together to honor Mary in ways that are scripturally based, evangelically motivated, liturgically appropriate, and ecumenically sensitive. Our hope in presenting this book to the wider church public is to celebrate Mary's singular dignity within the mystery of salvation, learning from her example what it means to magnify the Lord in total obedience and trust.

CARL E. BRAATEN
ROBERT W. JENSON

3. "The Magnificat," *Luther's Works*, vol. 21, pp. 326-29.
4. "The Hail Mary," *Luther's Works*, vol. 43, p. 39.
5. For example, "The One Mediator, the Saints, and Mary,"in *Lutherans and Catholics in Dialogue VIII*, ed. H. George Anderson, J. Francis Stafford, and Joseph A. Burgess (Minneapolis: Augsburg, 1992). See also *Mary in the New Testament*, ed. Raymond E. Brown, Karl P. Donfried, Joseph A. Fitzmyer, and John Reumann (Philadelphia: Fortress, 1978).

Most *Generations Shall Call Me Blessed:* *An Essay in Aid of a Grammar of Liturgy*

JAROSLAV PELIKAN

The source for the title of this essay is, of course, the Magnificat of the Virgin Mary from the first chapter of the Gospel according to Saint Luke in the Authorized Version of the English Bible (Luke 1:48), but rather presumptuously modified from her original formulation, "For behold, from henceforth *all* generations shall call me blessed," to "*most* generations," in order to take account of the statistical realities of modern church history, when she has certainly not always been called "blessed" by all generations. The source for its subtitle, much less familiar, is the most subtle, and in many respects the most problematical, of the writings of John Henry Cardinal Newman, his *Essay in Aid of a Grammar of Assent* of 1870 (the same year as the First Vatican Council!), also adjusted to take account of the primary venue within which the Church's reflection on the title of this theological conference, "Mary the Mother of God," has been carried on, which is worship and devotion. But Newman will be prominent here also through the counterpoint of the Mariological themes of the Liturgy — not, however, with his *Grammar of Assent,* nor with the passages on Mary in his devotional and homiletical works, as these have become available in a compilation published recently by Philip Boyce,[1] but with the work of his to which my lifelong debt has been the most profound, *An Essay on the Development of*

---

1. Philip Boyce, ed., *Mary: The Virgin Mary in the Life and Writings of John Henry Newman* (Grand Rapids: Eerdmans, 2001).

Christian Doctrine, both its original edition of 1845 and its heavily revised edition of 1878.[2]

Although elsewhere I have looked at the place of the Mother of God in the worship of the Western Church, especially the *Ave Maria* and the *Stabat mater dolorosa,*[3] I shall be drawing here upon the Eastern Liturgy.[4] That is not only because this happens to be how I pray, but also because one of the intriguing historical differences between East and West is that, in Newman's words, "the special prerogatives of St. Mary . . . were not fully recognized in the Catholic ritual till a late date."[5] Much of the devotion to the Mother of God initially traveled from East to West, as can be seen from the Mariology of Ambrose of Milan.[6] Such cherished Western Catholic treasures of Marian spirituality as the *Ave Maria,* the *Salve Regina,* and the *Stabat mater dolorosa,* moreover, stand largely on their own, as parts of the primarily nonliturgical private devotion and corporate worship of the West.[7] The East does have its parallels to all three of these: to the *Ave Maria* in such hymns as Богородице дево, which, as the sixth hymn in the Rachmaninoff setting of the *Vespers,* has become familiar to Western concert-goers especially through the recordings of the late Robert Shaw and of Mstislav Rostropovich (and which was sung in the devotions of this symposium); to the *Salve Regina,* for example, in "O victori-

---

2. Because most readers do not have easy access to the *editio princeps* of either of these, I cite the 1845 version (as *Essay 1845*) according to J. M. Cameron's edition (Harmondsworth: Pelican Books, 1974), and the 1878 version (as *Essay 1878*) according to the edition prepared and introduced by Ian Ker (Notre Dame: University of Notre Dame Press, 1989).

3. Jaroslav Pelikan, *Mary Through the Centuries: Her Place in the History of Culture* (New Haven: Yale University Press, 1996), pp. 125-36; but already in *The Riddle of Roman Catholicism* (Nashville: Abingdon, 1959), pp. 128-42.

4. I have adopted the versification — and quoted the Greek — of Anastasios Kallis, ed., *Liturgie: Die Göttliche Liturgie der Orthodoxen Kirche Deutsch-Griechisch-Kirchenslawisch* (Mainz: Matthias Grünewald Verlag, 1989), cited as "Kallis"; the English translation and its pagination come from *The Divine Liturgy According to St. John Chrysostom, with Appendices,* authorized by the Orthodox Church in America, 2nd ed. (South Canaan, Pa.: St. Tikhon's Seminary Press, 1977), cited as *OCA.*

5. Newman, *Essay 1845,* 389. By "Catholic," presumably though not necessarily, he means Western Catholic; so, at any rate, I am construing it in the present context.

6. Joseph Huhn, *Das Geheimnis der Jungfrau-Mutter Maria nach dem Kirchenvater Ambrosius* (Würzburg: Echter Verlag, 1954).

7. *Lexikon für Theologie und Kirche,*[3] 7:78-79.

ous leader of triumphant hosts!";[8] and to the *Stabat mater dolorosa* in the less well-known Θρῆνος Θεοτόκου of Romanos the Melodist.[9]

But the Eastern Orthodox tradition also makes a recurring address to Mary the Mother of God a more integral component of the central Eucharistic Liturgy itself. It seems to be at least an implicit recognition of this liturgical difference between East and West when the Second Vatican Council in *Lumen Gentium* "exhorts all the members of the Church generously to foster the cult, *especially the liturgical cult,* of the blessed Virgin," even as it acknowledges, in its curious (or curial) Latinity, "that people are not lacking among our separated sisters and brothers [*etiam inter fratres seiunctos non deesse*] . . . especially among Eastern Christians, who honor the Ever Virgin Mother of God with fervor and devotion."[10] And in a later decree, *Unitatis redintegratio,* the Council also asserts that "everyone knows with what great love the Christians of the East celebrate the Sacred Liturgy," in which, the Council continues, "the Christians of the East pay high tribute, in beautiful hymns, to Mary Ever Virgin."[11]

To learn how most generations have called her blessed, then, I propose to parse the grammar of the "fervor and devotion" in that "great love" and that "high tribute," as all of this is articulated in seven of the prayers and "beautiful hymns" of *The Divine Liturgy According to Saint John Chrysostom,* without being able for lack of space to do more than to cite here some of the many additional pertinent passages in other Orthodox liturgies, troparia, kontakia, and orders of worship. Just over a century ago, in his immensely popular and widely circulated *Das Wesen des Christentums* of 1900, Adolf von Harnack, allowing himself to make the shocking statement that "it was to destroy this sort of religion that Jesus Christ suffered himself to be nailed to the cross!" described the Orthodox Liturgy as "the cult of a mystery . . . , hundreds of efficacious formulas small and great, signs, pictures, and consecrated acts, which, if punctiliously and submissively observed, communicate divine grace and prepare the Christian for eternal life. Doctrine as such is for the most part some-

---

8. *OCA* 235.

9. Gregory W. Dobrov, "A Dialogue with Death: Ritual Lament and the *thrēnos Theotokou* of Romanos Melodos," *Greek, Roman, and Byzantine Studies* 35 (1994): 385-405.

10. Vatican II, *Lumen gentium,* 67, 69, *Decrees of the Ecumenical Councils,* 2 vols., ed. Norman P. Tanner et al. (Washington, D.C.: Georgetown University Press, 1990), 2:897-98; italics added. (Hereafter abbreviated as *DEC.*)

11. Vatican II, *Unitatis redintegratio,* 15, *DEC,* 2:916.

thing unknown; if it appears at all, it is only in the form of liturgical aphorisms."[12] But in the words of Anastasios Kallis in the Preface to his trilingual edition of the Liturgy in Greek, Church Slavonic, and German, "The identity of Orthodoxy consists neither in a [system of] doctrine, nor in an organizational structure, but in the correct praise of the Triune God, which has its center in the celebration of the Eucharist, or simply the Liturgy, through which a congregation assembled in the name of Christ becomes His body, becomes Church."[13] Whoever may have assembled the Liturgy in its present form and from whatever sources, which do seem to include more passages than was once thought from the writings of Saint John Chrysostom,[14] it would seem justifiable to draw here upon parallels to it in fourth-century Greek Christian thought, especially Athanasius and the three Cappadocians, for its interpretation.

As a theological methodology, using what Paul Oskar Kristeller called "sacred philology"[15] and probing the grammar of a sacred text to extract dogmatic meaning from it has the authoritative precedent both of Scripture and of Tradition, Western as well as Eastern. In Galatians 3, the apostle Paul, reasoning on the basis of the Greek singular τῷ σπέρματι σου in the Septuagint version of the promise to Abraham in Genesis (Gen. 12:7 LXX), "In thy seed shall all the nations of the earth be blessed" — where (as the RSV rendering of the passage with "your descendants" indicates) the Hebrew, and then the Greek, would seem to be a collective noun — declares: "He saith not, 'And to seeds,' as of many; but as of one, 'And to thy seed,' which is Christ."[16] In his *On the Holy Spirit,* written in 375 or so, Saint Basil of Caesarea is seeking to come to terms with the puzzling absence of explicit references in Scripture to the Holy Spirit as "God." To that end he employs several of what its most recent translator, David Anderson — in a rueful tone to which he was probably entitled af-

---

12. Adolf von Harnack, *What Is Christianity?* trans. Thomas Bailey Saunders. Reprint edition with introduction by Rudolf Bultmann (New York: Harper Torchbooks, [1900] 1957), pp. 237-38.

13. Kallis, ix.

14. G. Wagner, *Der Ursprung der Chrysostomusliturgie* (Münster: Liturgiegeschichtliche Quellen und Forschungen, 1973).

15. Paul Oskar Kristeller, *Renaissance Thought: The Classic, Scholastic, and Humanist Strains* (New York: Harper Torchbooks, 1961), p. 79.

16. Galatians 3:16 (AV), quoting the Authorized Version because of its more literal translation.

ter working his way through all that Cappadocian Greek — describes as "lengthy grammatical discussions in this treatise which surely bring frustration to reader and translator alike." Basil uses grammar, Anderson explains, to argue that "if saving regeneration begins through baptism in the name of Father, Son, and Spirit, with *name* in the singular, then Father, Son, and Spirit form a coordinate series, with all three sharing equal rank."[17] Likewise, in his *De Trinitate,* Saint Augustine of Hippo, with his training in Cicero and his unmatched sensitivity to the nuances of Latin grammar and rhetoric, parses the saying of Christ, "Ego et pater meus *unum* sumus" (John 10:30) — and not "*unus* sumus" — to point out that when "he has both said *unum* [neuter singular both in the Latin and in the original Greek] and *sumus* [plural, also in both Latin and Greek]," Christ is employing a grammatical anomaly with which only the orthodox dogma of the Trinity, by its distinction between the essence as singular and the persons as plural, is able to come to terms satisfactorily.[18]

Adverbial Participle of Means

Near the very beginning of the Divine Liturgy, and then at least three more times at various stages of it (as well as, for example, in Great Vespers), there occurs this hortatory prayer: "Commemorating our most holy, most pure, most blessed and glorious Lady Theotokos and ever Virgin Mary with all the saints, let us commend ourselves and each other, and all our life unto Christ our God."[19] Thus a participle, "commemorating," μνημονεύσαντες in Greek, which has "our most holy, most pure, most blessed and glorious Lady Theotokos and ever Virgin Mary" as its direct object in the genitive, is employed to modify a reflexive verb in the subjunctive, "let us commend ourselves," which has "Christ our God" as its indirect object in the dative. There are parallel grammatical constructions with the identical principal clause but with two different participial clauses near the close of the Liturgy: "Having asked for the unity of the Faith, and the communion of the Holy Spirit, let us commend ourselves

17. David Anderson, "Introduction" to *Saint Basil the Great on the Holy Spirit* (Crestwood, N.Y.: Saint Vladimir's Seminary Press, 1980), p. 11.

18. Augustine *On the Trinity* VII.vi.12 (*NPNF*-I 3:113).

19. I.A.2 (Kallis 49-51; *OCA* 31); again II.A.4 (Kallis 55; *OCA* 32); II.A.6 (Kallis 59; *OCA* 34); II.C (Kallis 113; *OCA* 59).

and each other, and all our life unto Christ our God";[20] and again, "Asking that this day may be without sin, let us commend ourselves and each other, and all our life unto Christ our God."[21] In the Great Commission of the New Testament, "Go therefore and make disciples of all nations, baptizing them in the name of the Father and of the Son and of the Holy Spirit, teaching them to observe all that I have commanded you,"[22] there is a similar grammatical construction of a participle modifying a command, with both "baptizing [βαπτίζοντες]" and "teaching [διδάσκοντες]" as what Ernest De Witt Burton (though without reference to the Great Commission) calls "the adverbial participle of means,"[23] modifying the main verb, the imperative "Make disciples [μαθητεύσατε]." Neither the baptizing nor the teaching is an end in itself, not even in the way that the making of disciples is. Obviously, the connection in the Great Commission is at once instrumental and yet inseparable, there being no means specified for making disciples, here in the Great Commission at any rate (whatever the methods of later missionaries may have been!), other than the teaching of the gospel and the administration of baptism.

So it is here in the grammar of the Liturgy. The absolute imperative, which is quite literally — and eternally — a matter of life and death, is that we "commend ourselves and each other, and all our life unto Christ our God." The Liturgy itemizes several adverbial participles of means identifying mutually complementary pathways to that indispensable goal, and in the following order: (1) that we "commemorate our most holy, most pure, most blessed and glorious Lady Theotokos and ever Virgin Mary"; (2) that we do so "with [μετά] all the saints"; (3) that we "ask for the unity of the Faith"; (4) that we "ask for the communion of the Holy Spirit"; and (5) that we "ask that this day may be without sin." The implication is that just as asking for the unity of the Faith and for the communion of the Holy Spirit and for protection from sin is not incompatible, but totally compatible, with commending ourselves and one another and all our life to Christ our God, because that is precisely how we do the commending, so also we do the commending to Christ by commemorat-

20. II.G.1 (Kallis 149; *OCA* 72-73).
21. II.I (*OCA* 84).
22. Matthew 28:19 (RSV).
23. Ernest De Witt Burton, *New Testament Moods and Tenses* (Chicago: University of Chicago Press, 1893), p. 171 (# 443).

ing Mary together with all the other saints. As for the very idea of such an incompatibility and therefore of the alleged conflict between loyalty to Christ and loyalty to His Mother, let me for now leave the polemic of *post hoc ergo propter hoc* to John Henry Newman, who does it so much better than I: "If we take a survey at least of Europe, we shall find that it is not those religious communions which are characterized by devotion towards the Blessed Virgin that have ceased to adore her Eternal Son, but those very bodies (when allowed by the law) which have renounced devotion to her."[24]

Metonymy:
The Son as Only-Begotten, the Mother as Ever-Virgin

Early in the Liturgy, as part of the preparation for the Little Entrance and the reading of the Epistle and Gospel lessons, there comes the following apostrophe, which was composed by the Emperor Justinian and is usually called "Μονογενής" from its opening words:

> *Only-begotten* Son and immortal Word of God,
> Who for our salvation didst will to be incarnate of Mary
>   the holy Theotokos and *Ever-virgin* Mary,
> Who without change didst become man and was crucified,
> O Christ our God, trampling down death by death,
> Who art one of the Holy Trinity, glorified with the Father
>   and the Holy Spirit,
> Save us![25]

It must be acknowledged that Emperor Justinian's dogmatic influence was not as great as that of the Emperor Constantine, with his sponsorship of the *homoousios;* but just as certainly, his dogmatic learning was greater.[26] For the present I am not examining, as I have done elsewhere,[27]

---

24. Newman, *Essay 1878*, 426.

25. I.A.5 (Kallis 57; *OCA* 34).

26. Kenneth Paul Wesche, ed. and trans., *On the Person of Christ: The Christology of Emperor Justinian* (Crestwood, N.Y.: Saint Vladimir's Seminary Press, 1991).

27. Jaroslav Pelikan, *The Spirit of Eastern Christendom (600-1700)* (Chicago: University of Chicago Press, 1974), p. 42.

whether, and to what extent, the formulation of the paradoxes of the Incarnation here — in the juxtaposition of the phrases "who art One of the Holy Trinity" and "Immortal Logos" with the phrase "trampling down death by death," which is reminiscent of the controversies over the phrase "One of the Trinity was crucified on our behalf"[28] — reflects Justinian's own Christological tilt, as this is articulated in his *Edict* of 551. Rather, what interests me here is the subtle but I think unavoidable metonymy implicit in the use of the two technical terms, the Christological Only-Begotten and the Mariological Ever-Virgin. This Johannine "title of majesty,"[29] μονογενής, is a Greek term whose ancestry goes all the way back to the concluding words of Plato's *Timaeus*, εἷς οὐρανὸς ὅδε μονογενὴς ὤν which Benjamin Jowett translates as "the one only-begotten heaven," but which, for example, R. G. Bury in the Loeb Classical Library renders with "sole of its kind."[30] Modern New Testament scholars and translators have sought to scale down its meaning from "only-begotten" to "only," and therefore to treat it as just a little more than another word for μόνος.[31] Whatever may be the philological validity of that effort, it does seem clear that to the later tradition which composed the Liturgy and the dogmatic decrees of the Councils, what made the Son of God μόνος, "single," was this, that He was, in the precise and technical sense, μονογενής, "only-begotten." In that tradition it was a standard theological practice, as can be seen for example in Hilary of Poitiers, to draw out what I once called "the congruence of the immanent and the economic"[32] and the paradoxical parallelism in the relations between the divine and the human begetting or birth of the Incarnate Son of God. A fitting corollary of that congruence and paradoxical parallelism was the teaching that the human birth as well as the divine birth was unique, so that He was the single and only-begotten Son of God but also the single and only-begotten Son of Mary — which

28. Werner Elert, *Der Ausgang der altkirchlichen Christologie* (Berlin: Lutherisches Verlagshaus, 1957), pp. 71-132.

29. Ferdinand Hahn, *Christologische Hoheitstitel im frühen Christentum* (Göttingen: Vandenhoeck und Ruprecht, 1963).

30. Plato, *Timaeus* 92C.

31. William F. Arndt and F. Wilbur Gingrich, eds., *A Greek-English Lexicon of the New Testament and Other Early Christian Literature,* 2nd ed. (Chicago: University of Chicago Press, 1979), p. 527.

32. Jaroslav Pelikan, *Development of Christian Doctrine: Some Historical Prolegomena* (New Haven: Yale University Press, 1969), pp. 131-36.

meant that she was not only παρθένος, Virgin, but ἀειπαρθένος, Ever-Virgin, as the Second Council of Constantinople decreed in 553.[33]

And if we read verse eighteen of the first chapter of the Fourth Gospel as saying, "No one has ever seen God; but *the only-begotten God* [μονογενὴς θεός], he who is nearest to the Father's heart, he has made him known," the metonymy becomes even more striking.[34] That reading follows the consistent usage of the Cappadocian Fathers as well as a body of New Testament manuscript evidence impressive enough to warrant the judgment of one textual scholar that "more and more critical texts have adopted *theos;* however, commentators and translators have been generally reluctant to accept that reading as the original or as the better of the two available readings."[35] On the basis of the New Testament declaration that "every fatherhood *in heaven and on earth*" is named from the Fatherhood of God[36] — rather than the other way around, as a commonsensical (or Freudian) reductionism would suppose, namely, that we call God "Our Father who art in heaven" because of our earthly fathers — Saint Athanasius and the Cappadocians consistently maintain that the real metonymies and metaphors of theology lie in attributing to creatures, as antitypes, the realities, hypostases, attributes, and energies of God the Holy Trinity as prototypes[37] — an insight for whose modern restatement we are indebted above all to Karl Barth.[38] Then it would seem to make sense that the metonymy is to be defined as follows: the ontological title "the only-begotten God," applied by Saint John the Theologian to the preexistent Second Hypostasis in the Trinity, has as its corollary in the di-

---

33. *DEC* 1:116.

34. John 1:18; Jaroslav Pelikan, *What Has Athens to Do with Jerusalem? "Timaeus" and "Genesis" in Counterpoint* (Ann Arbor: University of Michigan Press, 1997), pp. 101-04.

35. Paul R. McReynolds, "John 1:18 in Textual Variation and Translation," in *New Testament Textual Criticism, Its Significance for Exegesis: Essays in Honor of Bruce M. Metzger,* ed. Eldon J. Epp and Gordon D. Fee (Oxford: Oxford University Press, 1981), p. 105.

36. Ephesians 3:15.

37. Jaroslav Pelikan, *The Light of the World: A Basic Image in Early Christian Thought* (New York: Harper and Brothers, 1962), p. 32; Jaroslav Pelikan, *Christianity and Classical Culture: The Metamorphosis of Natural Theology in the Christian Encounter with Hellenism* (New Haven: Yale University Press, 1993), pp. 87-89.

38. Karl Barth, *Church Dogmatics,* I-1, *The Doctrine of the Word of God,* trans. G. T. Thomson (Edinburgh: T. & T. Clark, 1936), p. 451.

vine economy of the Incarnation the ecclesiastical title "Ever-Virgin" for Mary the Theotokos. It is an application of the same metonymy and parallelism, therefore, when at the Meeting of Our Lord Jesus Christ in the Temple on 2 February, the special Hymn to the Theotokos sings: "We also magnify the first-begotten Son of the unoriginate Father, the first-born Son of the unwedded Mother!"[39]

A Holy Homonym:
The Thrice-Holy One and the Holy Theotokos

One of the special high points of the Orthodox Liturgy is the Trisagion, which is sung three times: "Holy God, Holy Mighty, Holy Immortal: have mercy on us!"[40] It is prayed privately as well as liturgically, and often inscribed for an Orthodox burial on the shroud or on a headband worn by the body of the deceased. Like the Sanctus of the Western Mass — which the Eastern Liturgy also includes, but at another place, namely, the Eucharistic Prayer[41] — the Trisagion is a kind of liturgical Midrash on the "Holy, Holy, Holy" hymn of the seraphim in the inaugural vision of Isaiah (Isa. 6:3).[42] But because English usage here, as well as in the related terms "justify" and "righteousness," fluctuates between the Germanic and the Latinate origins of the language and makes distinctions between the terms *holy* and *saint* and *sanctify* that can obscure the connections, while the Greek uses ἅγιος and its cognates throughout (plus ὁσιότης once), it may clarify the language to cite the Trisagion and its surrounding prayer by inserting the original Greek (transliterated) of those terms: "*Hagios* God, *hagios* mighty, *hagios* immortal: have mercy on us. O God the *hagios,* who dost rest in the *hagioi,* . . . *hagiason* our souls and bodies, and enable us to serve Thee in *hosiotēs* all the days of our life. Through the intercessions of the *hagia* Theotokos and of all the *hagioi* who from the beginning of the world have been well-pleasing to Thee. . . . For *hagios* art Thou, O our God."[43] Similarly, the response to the announcement

---

39. *OCA* 234.

40. I.C.1-2 (Kallis 67; *OCA* 39).

41. F.1.2 (Kallis 127; *OCA* 63).

42. See Anton Baumstark, "Trishagion und Qeduscha," *Jahrbuch für Liturgiewissenschaft* 3 (1923): 18-32.

43. I.C.1-2 (Kallis 67-69; *OCA* 38-39).

(which goes back to the early church), "The holy things are for the holy!" is the exclusivistic-sounding formulation "*One is holy,* one is Lord, Jesus Christ,"[44] not as though it were mistaken to speak of "holy" things or of "holy" people, for whom these holy things are set aside, but because the "holiness" both of the Church and of the Sacraments, and above all that of the "holy" Theotokos, is derivative from the essential holiness of God, which does not make it any the less real, but to the contrary guarantees that it *is* real. This is what Newman has in mind when he speaks about the principle of "created mediation."[45]

Zeugma of the Preposition ἐκ

Anyone who brings to the exegetical study of the Orthodox Liturgy a detailed knowledge of the Latin Mass and who heeds the repeated warning, "Let us be attentive!" should be particularly attentive to the way the Holy Spirit is spoken of, not only in the controversial *Filioque* of Article 8 of the Creed but already in Article 3 of the Creed: "And was incarnate from the Holy Spirit and the Virgin Mary [ἐκ Πνεύματος ἁγίου καὶ Μαρίας τῆς Παρθένου]."[46] This is a use of the Classical rhetorical figure of zeugma, in which the single preposition ἐκ is employed only once, but is meant in two quite distinct but closely connected senses. (A colleague in Classics illustrates the figure of zeugma with the sentence: "She arrived in a huff and a Cadillac.") By contrast, the Latin Mass (as well as the English liturgical versions of the Creed, Protestant as well as Roman Catholic, that have been translated directly from the Latin rather than from the Greek) casts that passage to read: "Et incarnatus est *de* Spiritu Sancto *ex* Maria virgine." The conjunction καί/*et* is omitted, and therefore there is no zeugma. Instead, the preposition *ex*, corresponding to the Greek ἐκ, is applied only to Mary; and for the role of the Holy Spirit in the Incarnation the Latin text introduces a new preposition, *de,* for which there is no equivalent in the Greek text of the First Council of Constantinople of 381, at any rate as this has been transmitted by the Council of Chalcedon of 451 (the original creedal decree of 381 having been lost). The usage of

44. II.G.4 (Kallis 157; *OCA* 75).
45. Newman, *Essay* 1878, 138.
46. II.E (Kallis 119; *OCA* 61).

prepositions in this clause or its equivalent varies among the early creeds in intriguing, if not always totally explicable ways, which may help to account for the difference between the two ways that the *Constantinopolitanum* has been transmitted. Written in Greek but preserved only in a Latin translation, the creed that appears in *The Apostolic Tradition* of Hippolytus of Rome contains the same phrase, "qui natus est *de* Spiritu Sancto *ex* Maria virgine," whatever the original Greek may have read; this is also the combination of prepositions recorded by Ambrose of Milan and by Rufinus of Aquileia.[47] But the Western tradition, which is best known for the use not only of two prepositions but of two passive participles in the eventual *textus receptus* of the Apostles' Creed, "conceived by the Holy Spirit, born of the Virgin Mary," is not monolithic. For Augustine, in at least one of his several quite divergent versions of the Creed, reads "*de* Spiritu Sancto *et* virgine Maria," thus preserving the zeugma of 381,[48] whereas in another version he says "de Spiritu Sancto *ex* virgine Maria."[49] As is well known, the Creed of Nicaea of 325 does not refer to the birth from Mary at all; but *The Niceno-Constantinopolitan Creed* does. The Greek reads as I have quoted it, employing a single preposition with the two objects; but the Latin translation follows the Western usage cited from Hippolytus and Ambrose. It was in recognition of her unique role in the Divine Economy of the Incarnation, a role so utterly unique that there is nothing unseemly or blasphemous about the creedal zeugma yoking the divine Person of the Holy Spirit and the human person of the Virgin Mary, that she was named Theotokos by the Council of Ephesus in 431 — not only a "logical sequence," in Newman's terminology, for the fifth of his original criteria of the development of doctrine, but "an addition," as he goes on to acknowledge much later in the *Essay on Development, "greater perhaps than any before or since,* to the letter of the primitive faith."[50]

---

47. Heinrich Denzinger, ed., *Enchiridion symbolorum definitionum et declarationum de rebus fidei et morum* [1854], 37th ed., ed. Peter Hünermann (Freiburg im Breisgau: Herder, 1991), 10; 13; 16. (Hereafter cited as "Denzinger," by paragraph number).

48. Denzinger, 14.

49. Denzinger, 21.

50. Newman, *Essay* 1845, 109; 319; italics added.

Adverb of Genus and Species:
Not So Much Exception as Exemplar

Certainly the most ample and extravagant of all the apostrophes to Mary the Theotokos in *The Divine Liturgy According to Saint John Chrysostom* is the hymn of choir and congregation: "It is truly meet to bless you, O Theotokos, ever-blessed and most pure, and the Mother of our God. More honorable than the Cherubim, and more glorious than the Seraphim: without defilement you gave birth to God the Word: true Theotokos, we magnify you."[51] Variations on this hymn and elaborations of it recur in the special liturgies for several of the festivals associated with the Theotokos: at the Feast of the Theophany on 6 January, "Magnify, O my soul, the most pure Theotokos, more honorable than the heavenly hosts! No tongue is capable of praising you worthily: the angelic mind is overawed in exalting you, O Theotokos";[52] again at the Feast of the Meeting in the Temple on 2 February, "Rejoice, O Virgin Theotokos, Full of Grace! From you shone the Sun of Righteousness, Christ our God, enlightening those who sat in darkness!";[53] yet again at the Feast of the Annunciation on 25 March, "O victorious leader of triumphant hosts!";[54] and finally at the Feast of the Dormition of the Theotokos on 15 August, commemorated in the West as the Feast of the Assumption,[55] "The limits of nature are overcome in you, O Pure Virgin: for birthgiving remains virginal and life is united to death!"[56] The words of these praises of the Theotokos are echoed in the second stanza of the Anglican hymn, "Ye Watchers and Ye Holy Ones," by John Athelstan Laurie Riley (1858-1945), who was a widely traveled student of the Eastern churches and the author of a book about Mount Athos, *Athos, or the Mountain of the Monks* (London, 1887):[57]

O higher than the cherubim,
More glorious than the seraphim,

51. II.F.6 (Kallis 137-39; *OCA* 68-69).
52. *OCA* 232.
53. *OCA* 233.
54. *OCA* 235.
55. Brian E. Daley, ed. and trans., *On the Dormition of Mary: Early Patristic Homilies* (Crestwood, N.Y.: Saint Vladimir's Seminary Press, 1998).
56. *OCA* 242.
57. John Julian, *A Dictionary of Hymnology* (reprint ed. New York: Dover Publications, [1907] 1957), 2:1692-93.

Lead their praises, Alleluia!
Thou bearer of the eternal Word,
Most gracious, Magnify the Lord.

This hymn appears in the hymnals of many Protestant churches where, as I have often said, the same words about Mary, if used in the prose of a sermon, might well evoke the familiar accusation of "Mariolatry." But any such accusation ignores the grammatical context; for these epithets, "More honorable than the Cherubim, and more glorious beyond compare than the Seraphim," come in response to a general intercession by the congregation on behalf of *all* the faithful departed, of whom she is one: "Again we offer unto Thee this reasonable worship for those who have fallen asleep in the faith: ancestors, fathers, patriarchs, prophets, apostles, preachers, evangelists, martyrs, confessors, ascetics, and every righteous spirit made perfect in faith. Especially [ἐξαιρέτως] for our most holy, most pure, most blessed and glorious Lady Theotokos and ever-virgin Mary."[58] For amid all the rhapsodic and pleonastic language about the relation between the cosmological position of the Theotokos and that of the most sublime of all the members of the angelic hierarchy as they are catalogued in the celestial cartography of Dionysius the Areopagite, the emphasis is on the total genus of those who have fallen asleep in the faith, and then, within that genus, on the special case of the Theotokos. The concern in this characterization is not so much with Mary as an *exception,* as it is in the famous passage in Saint Augustine's *Nature and Grace,* which was to run a dialectical course with the no less famous passage in Saint Bernard's *Epistle to the Canons of Lyons* throughout the stormy history of the development of the Western doctrine of the Immaculate Conception during the later Middle Ages.[59] Rather, it is on her as *example,* or more precisely as the preeminent *exemplar,* of how the grace of God deals with human freedom. Therefore the roll call of those who have fallen asleep in the faith reaches its climax with the adverb ἐξαιρέτως, meaning "picked out, selected, chosen,"[60] which both sets her apart as the special object of God's predestinating choice and

58. II.F.6 (Kallis 137-39; *OCA* 68-69).

59. Jaroslav Pelikan, *Reformation of Church and Dogma (1300-1700)* (Chicago: University of Chicago Press, 1984), pp. 38-50.

60. Geoffrey Lampe, ed., *A Patristic Greek Lexicon* (Oxford: Clarendon Press, 1961), pp. 490-91.

election (as she is also in Luther's Christmas hymn, "Vom Himmel hoch," where the angel calls her "eine Jungfrau *auserkoren*") and puts her into continuity with every other "righteous spirit made perfect in faith" who has fallen asleep down to the present. The Annunciation [εὐαγγελισμός] of the Theotokos became in Byzantine theology the supreme case study of the mysterious relation between this predestinating divine choice and the inviolable human freedom expressed in her sublime confession and expression of faith in the Word of God. As Newman summarizes them, the Greek Fathers in their bold treatment of the Annunciation "taught that, as the first woman might have foiled the Tempter and did not, so *had Mary been disobedient or unbelieving on Gabriel's message, the Divine Economy would have been frustrated.*"[61]

Metaphor of History of Salvation: The Theotokos as New Jerusalem

At every celebration of the Divine Liturgy, and with many repetitions especially during the Paschal Vigil and elsewhere, the Theotokos is addressed in the following acclamation, whose authorship is attributed to Saint John of Damascus: "Shine! Shine! O New Jerusalem! The glory of the Lord has shone on you! Exult now and be glad, O Zion! Be radiant, O Pure Theotokos, in the Resurrection of your Son!"[62] It bears pointing out that the metaphor being invoked here is not the more common one, "*Daughter of* Zion," employed by both Isaiah and Zechariah and familiar from the Gospel account of the Entry into Jerusalem on Palm Sunday,[63] which I have used to underscore the tragically forgotten bond between Mary and the Jewish tradition,[64] but simply "Zion" and even "New Jerusalem." In the tortuous history of how Christians have invoked the metaphors of "the Holy City" and of "the Land called Holy," as that history has been so fruitfully examined by Robert Wilken,[65] this metaphoric in-

61. Newman, *Essay 1845*, 389; italics added.
62. II.II (Kallis 175; *OCA* 82).
63. Isaiah 62:11; Zechariah 9:9; Matthew 21:5.
64. Pelikan, *Mary Through the Centuries*, pp. 23-36.
65. Robert L. Wilken, *The Land Called Holy: Palestine in Christian History and Thought* (New Haven: Yale University Press, 1992).

termingling of the Holy City and the Holy Theotokos holds a special place, and its components deserve careful examination.

The fundamental component of this metaphor of the history of salvation is the centrality of the event of the Resurrection, not only when these verses are used in the Paschal season but whenever they are sung: "Exult now and be glad, O Zion! Be radiant, O Pure Theotokos, *in the Resurrection of your Son* [ἐν τῇ ἐγέρσει τοῦ τόκου σου]!" At each crucial stage of the history of salvation from its beginning to its climax, she is present: she "magnified the Lord" at the Annunciation of the Nativity of her Son who is the Son of God, and now she "exults" and "is glad" and "is radiant at the Resurrection of your Son." In this "exulting" at His Resurrection, moreover, she is seen not only as an individual, nor only as "above all creatures, O Pure One," as she is hailed in the celebration of the Annunciation,[66] but as, almost in the Emersonian sense of the word, the Representative, and therefore as a corporate reality and the Second Eve. But just as in the Cherubic Hymn, introducing the Great Entrance, the worshiping congregation is said to consist of those "who mystically represent [εἰκονίζοντες] the Cherubim,"[67] so she "iconizes" and is representative not only of the new humanity but of the old Holy City, the Jerusalem that hailed her Son with Hosannas and "Blessed is he that comes in the name of the Lord" on Palm Sunday, that rejected him on Good Friday, and that now, through her, is the New Jerusalem and Zion, yet in that mysterious and unbreakable continuity with the Old that is the theme of Romans 9–11 — and "radiant at the Resurrection of her Son."

Benediction Expressed through an Instrumental Dative

Even at the end of worship, the presence of Mary is made explicit, and that through what Greek grammarians call an instrumental dative, performing the same function as the Latin ablative. Where Western services, whether Roman Catholic or Protestant, usually pronounce the Aaronitic blessing of Numbers 6:24-26 or the Apostolic blessing of 2 Corinthians 13:14 or the Trinitarian blessing "Benedictio omnipotentis Dei," the Orthodox Liturgy pronounces: "May He who rose from the dead, Christ our

66. *OCA* 235.
67. II.B.1 (Kallis 97; *OCA* 52).

true God, *through the prayers of His most pure Mother* [ταῖς πρεσβείσις τῆς παναχράντου αὐτοῦ μητρός] . . . of the holy and righteous Ancestors of God, Joachim and Anna; and of all the saints: have mercy on us, and save us, for He is good and loves mankind."[68] This instrumental dative, "through the prayers of His most pure Mother," recalls the familiar closing words of the *Ave Maria,* "Ora pro nobis peccatoribus, nunc et in hora mortis nostrae!" and fittingly encapsulates the entire system of reliance on what, as I have noted earlier, Newman calls "created mediation."

Once again, the grammar of the Liturgy carefully keeps the relationships straight. This Benediction speaks unmistakably about intercession, specifying that the mercy and blessing and salvation being pronounced upon the congregation are "through the prayers of His most pure Mother" and of the other saints. Therefore there is an intercession referred to here that is somehow distinct from that of Christ, who, as Saint Paul says, "is even at the right hand of God, who also maketh intercession for us."[69] For here the one "who also maketh intercession for us" is His Mother, whose continuing prayer is said to be efficacious, not only for this Benediction but for the welfare of the Church as a whole and of its individual members "nunc et in hora mortis nostrae."

Despite the quite remarkable compilation of passages from Luther, Calvin, Zwingli, and Bullinger that Walter Tappolet has collected under the title *The Reformers in Praise of Mary,*[70] it is clear that this notion of the ongoing intercessory prayer of Mary and the saints — scandalous as it had undoubtedly sometimes become in the later Middle Ages, through a deadly mixture of superstition, heresy, and commercialization — was singled out as a special object of criticism in the confessions of the Protestant Reformation.[71] The *Geneva Confession* of 1536, citing the Lord's Prayer as the divinely given model of how to pray, asserts, in opposition to Catholic doctrine and practice: "We reject the intercession of the saints as a superstition invented by men contrary to Scripture, for the reason that it proceeds from mistrust of the sufficiency of the intercession of Jesus

68. II.J.3 (Kallis 187; *OCA* 87).

69. Romans 8:34 (AV); also Hebrews 7:25.

70. Walter Tappolet, *Das Marienlob der Reformatoren* (Tübingen: Katzmann Verlag, 1962).

71. I quote several sentences here from chapter 6 of my book, *Credo: Historical and Theological Guide to Creeds and Confessions of Faith in the Christian Tradition* (New Haven: Yale University Press, 2003).

Christ."[72] The *French Confession* makes the same point, and also cites the Lord's Prayer in substantiation: "We believe, as Jesus Christ is our only Advocate, and as He commands us to ask of the Father in His name, and as it is not lawful for us to pray except in accordance with the model God has taught us by His Word, that all imaginations of men concerning the intercession of dead saints are an abuse and a device of Satan [*abus et fallace de Satan*] to lead men from the right way of worship."[73] The *Augsburg Confession* puts its criticism of the invocation of the saints somewhat more mildly, contenting itself with the objection that "it cannot be proved from the Scriptures that we are to invoke saints or seek help from them."[74] In explanation of this criticism, the *Apology of the Augsburg Confession* concedes, more mildly still, "that the saints in heaven pray for the Church in general, as they prayed for the Church Universal while they were on earth"; but even this concession not only is qualified by the stipulation that such praying applies only to "the Church *in general*," rather than to our specific day-by-day needs, but is accompanied by the insistence that this prayer *by* the departed saints, including the Virgin Mary, cannot be used to justify our prayer *to* the departed saints, including prayers to her, asking that they pray for us.[75]

It is a recognition of this historical circumstance, that — while most generations have called her blessed and have prayed for her intercessory prayer, others have not, and do not — this symposium of the Center for Catholic and Evangelical Theology dedicates itself to the proposition that "Evangelical" and "Catholic" (and, for that matter, "Orthodox") are not in the first instance labels of denominations or theological parties at all, but mutually reinforcing norms, also in the praise of "Mary the Mother of God."

72. *Geneva Confession* 12-13; also *Geneva Catechism* 238.
73. *Confessio Gallica* 24.
74. *Augsburg Confession* [German] 21.2; also *Smalcald Articles* 2.2.26.
75. *Apology of the Augsburg Confession* 21.9.

18

"Nothing Will Be Impossible with God": Mary as the Mother of Believers

BEVERLY ROBERTS GAVENTA

Several years ago I delivered an address at an ecumenical conference at Princeton Theological Seminary. As I prepared for that occasion, I astonished myself by writing — and then I astonished a number of other people by saying in public — that the time had come for Protestants to join with Catholic and Orthodox Christians in addressing Mary as Mother of Believers. On that occasion, I confess, the statement emerged as something of a rhetorical flourish. I wanted to challenge my Protestant colleagues and myself to give attention to Mary, to move beyond saying what we do *not* believe in order to articulate what we *do* believe.[1] Now, however, I find that I can return to what was a rhetorical flourish and make it with real confidence. In Luke's Gospel, at the Annunciation to Mary, Luke also announces what becomes a (perhaps even *the*) central theme of his two volumes: "Nothing will be impossible with God" (1:37 NRSV). Mary's response signals her consent to the role of the Mother of Jesus. In addition, it identifies another central theme, that of the consent of human beings to God's will. When she consents to God's will, Mary becomes the Mother of Believers.

It should be clear already that this proposal about identifying Mary as Mother of Believers differs substantially from more traditional propos-

---

1. That essay was published under the title, "'All Generations Will Call Me Blessed': Mary in Biblical and Ecumenical Perspective," in *The Princeton Seminary Bulletin* 18 (1997): 250-61.

19

als about that title. John 19 customarily serves as the beginning place for identifying Mary as the symbolic mother of the church, as she becomes the mother of the Beloved Disciple.[2] A second line of thinking about the motherhood of Mary begins from the image of the church as the body of Christ. Here the reasoning is as follows: if Mary is the mother of Jesus, and Jesus is the head of his body the church, then Mary is the mother of the church as well.[3] The proposal I am making draws instead entirely on Luke-Acts and therefore makes an additional argument for the title Mother of Believers. It may also be important to note that I come to this proposal from a Reformed tradition that, at least in recent years, has manifested little or no interest in Mary. A single piece of evidence should tell the tale: the "Brief Statement of Faith" issued by the Presbyterian Church USA in 1991 lifts up Sarah, but it makes no reference, direct or indirect, to Mary the Mother of Jesus.

Mary in the New Testament

Before turning to Luke-Acts, a brief reminder of the slender appearances of Mary in the New Testament may be beneficial. The letters of Paul mention Mary not at all, apart from the reference to Jesus' birth in Galatians 4:4: "when the fulfillment of time came, God sent his son, born of a woman, born under the Law."[4] In its context, the verse states only that Jesus is born to a Jewish woman (see also Rom. 1:3; 9:5). Even on the most generous interpretation, however, that Jesus is "born of a woman" says little about the particular woman or her significance.

Mark's Gospel mentions Mary only twice, first when the family of Jesus, believing him to be mad, attempts to restrain him (Mark 3:31-35), and again when the tongues of the Nazareth neighbors begin to wag:

2. See, for example, Arthur Burton Calkins, "Mary's Spiritual Maternity," in *Mary Is for Everyone,* ed. William McLoughlin, OSM, and Jill Pinnock (Leominster, Mass.: Gracewing, 1997), pp. 68-85. For a discussion of the exegetical problems, see Raymond E. Brown, *The Gospel According to John (xiii–xxi),* Anchor Bible 29A (Garden City, N.Y.: Doubleday, 1970), pp. 922-27; *The Death of the Messiah: From Gethsemane to the Grave,* 2 vols., Anchor Bible Reference Library (New York: Doubleday, 1994), 2:1019-26.

3. Calkins, "Mary's Spiritual Maternity."

4. All biblical translations are my own unless otherwise indicated.

"Isn't this the carpenter, the son of Mary and the brother of James and Joses and Judas and Simon? Aren't his sisters here with us?" (6:3).[5]

The Gospel of Matthew introduces Mary at the conclusion of a genealogy in which four other women precede her, and what a collection they are: Tamar, Rahab, Ruth, and the "wife of Uriah"! Placing Mary in such dubious company, Matthew then tells the story of the threat posed to Mary and her unborn child by Joseph's concern for his own good name and the threat posed later by Herod's determination to protect his throne. Matthew connects Mary with that threat to Jesus, at every point linking her name to his, yet in all this Mary herself never opens her mouth.[6]

In the Fourth Gospel, of course, Mary does speak, and it is an enigmatic speech indeed, as "the mother of Jesus" announces at a wedding in Cana that the wine supply has been exhausted and then, following Jesus' even more enigmatic response, she tells the stewards to do whatever Jesus instructs. (Where the hosts for this wedding have disappeared to, that Mary and Jesus are in charge of the refreshment table, is yet another exegetical mystery.) The "mother of Jesus" returns at the crucifixion, where she stands as witness and then receives the Beloved Disciple as her child and he in turn receives her as his mother.[7]

Each of these treatments of Mary bears close examination, as each conforms closely to the overall design of the larger work. Mary may be a minor character from a literary point of view, but in every case she represents *in nuce* some important facet of the Gospel. Also, each of these treatments helps readers to think about Mary in very particular ways. In this paper, however, instead of surveying the field, I want to focus on Luke, who of course gives more attention to Mary than does any other New Testament writer. And what I will contend is this: in the exchange between

5. Slender though Mark's references to Mary may be, E. Elizabeth Johnson sees in them an example of the gospel's radical disorientation and reorientation of family life; see "'Who Is My Mother?': Family Values in the Gospel of Mark," in *Blessed One: Protestant Perspectives on Mary,* ed. Beverly Roberts Gaventa and Cynthia L. Rigby (Louisville: West-minster/John Knox, 2002), pp. 32-46.

6. This paragraph summarizes my discussion of the Matthean Mary in *Mary: Glimpses of the Mother of Jesus,* Studies on Personalities of the New Testament (Columbia, S.C.: University of South Carolina Press, 1995; Minneapolis: Fortress, 1999), pp. 29-48.

7. On the mother of Jesus in John, see *Mary: Glimpses of the Mother of Jesus,* pp. 79-99.

Gabriel and Mary, we see Mary as the recipient of the gospel's central claim and not only as the first disciple but as the mother of disciples.

Mary in Luke-Acts

Since the 1978 volume, *Mary in the New Testament,* it has become a commonplace to refer to the Lukan Mary as the first disciple. In that significant volume, a panel of Catholic and Protestant scholars characterized the Lukan Mary as "the first Christian disciple" and as a "model" for disciples. They found Luke's treatment of Mary consistent from its beginning at the annunciation to its end in Mary's appearance with the Eleven at the Upper Room.[8] Following the publication of that volume, Raymond Brown and Joseph Fitzmyer (both of whom were involved in the earlier work), in their respective commentaries, elaborated on the notion that Luke's consistent presentation of Mary is that of an ideal disciple. In Brown's words, "Mary . . . responds obediently to God's word from the first as a representative of the Anawim of Israel (1:38); she appears in the ministry as a representative of the ideals of true discipleship . . . ; and she endures till Pentecost to become a Christian and a member of the Church. . . ."[9]

The influence of this viewpoint may be measured by attempts to modify it. In *The Illegitimacy of Jesus,* Jane Schaberg concedes that Luke portrays Mary as an ideal disciple, but she attributes this motif to Luke's need to defend Mary's honor against the tradition of Jesus' illegitimate conception.[10] Richard Horsley, in *The Liberation of Christmas,* interprets Mary as representative of those who are "the lowly," not only in a spiritual sense but in "concrete socioeconomic and political" terms.[11]

In my own earlier work on the Lukan portrait of Mary, I identified not one but three distinct roles associated with Mary in Luke-Acts. In re-

8. *Mary in the New Testament: A Collaborative Assessment by Protestant and Roman Catholic Scholars,* ed. Raymond E. Brown, Karl P. Donfried, Joseph A. Fitzmyer, and John Reumann (Philadelphia: Fortress/New York: Paulist, 1978), pp. 105-77.

9. Raymond E. Brown, *The Birth of the Messiah: A Commentary on the Infancy Narratives in Matthew and Luke* (Garden City, N.Y.: Doubleday, 1977), p. 499; Joseph A. Fitzmyer, *The Gospel According to Luke I–IX,* Anchor Bible 28 (Garden City, N.Y.: Doubleday, 1981), p. 341.

10. San Francisco: Harper and Row, 1987.

11. (New York: Crossroad, 1989), p. 111.

sponse to the annunciation of Jesus' birth, Mary does appear as the *first disciple.* Her affirmation, "Behold, the slave of the Lord. Let it be to me according to your word," provides her assent to the gospel. Elizabeth's praise of Mary's confidence in God's word reinforces her role as a true disciple. With the powerful words of the Magnificat, she becomes not only a disciple, but also a *prophet.* Its imagery of God's exalting of the lowly and humbling of the mighty recalls prophetic themes and anticipates the presence of those same themes in Jesus' sermon at Nazareth. Mary's third role in Luke-Acts, that of *mother,* appears to be her most direct and obvious, but in fact it emerges as the most complex. (That, of course, may be true for all of us who are parents — it is our most complex role.) Luke provides little description of the actual birth of Jesus, the point at which Mary becomes a mother. The story provides scant glorification of Mary, since its focus everywhere is the baby rather than the mother. And yet at several points Luke distinguishes Mary and her response to events from those others who are also present. Mary is the one who ponders the things that have happened, both in response to the shepherds' visit and following the uniquely Lukan scene in which the adolescent Jesus is teaching temple authorities (2:19, 51). According to the oracle of Simeon, it is Mary's soul that will be pierced (2:35a). It is Mary who announces her anguish over the disappearance of Jesus following the Passover trip to Jerusalem (2:48). These brief notices serve several functions in the narrative, one of which is to capture the very normal attachment of mother to child.[12]

The Annunciation to Mary

Against that background of the larger Lukan treatment of Mary, I want to revisit Luke's presentation, focusing especially on the exchange between Mary and Gabriel and its significance for Luke's larger narrative program. Luke identifies Mary with the leanest of descriptions, especially when considered against the role about to be handed her. He introduces her by means of a report that Gabriel is sent by God to Nazareth in Galilee to "a

12. For more detail, see *Mary: Glimpses of the Mother of Jesus,* pp. 49-78. Although I have distinguished these three roles (that of disciple, prophet, and mother) from one another in order to clarify each of them, they are in fact significantly connected with one another. Unless we see all of these, we will once again flatten Mary's character and reduce her to a single feature or one function.

virgin engaged to a man by the name of Joseph, from the house of David, and the name of the virgin is Mary" (1:26-27). By stunning contrast with his introductions of Elizabeth and Zechariah, Luke says not a word about Mary's righteousness, her faithfulness to the Law, or her family of origin (see 1:5-25). Nothing in the introduction of Mary qualifies her for this role apart from God's own favor dispensed to her. That unqualified statement about Mary appears to ignore the longstanding debate about Gabriel's initial greeting (that is, does "favored one" and later "you have found favor" presuppose that Mary has merit of her own before God? Or do these expressions point forward to what God is about to do?). That debate can flourish, at least in part, *because* Luke provides readers with no other basis for discerning Mary's credentials.[13] To put it directly, one of the reasons interpreters find themselves at odds over the precise nuance of Gabriel's greeting is that Luke gives readers little else by way of introducing Mary.

Gabriel makes his announcement: Mary will conceive and bear a son whom she is to name Jesus:

> "He will be great, and will be called the Son of the Most High, and the Lord God will give to him the throne of his ancestor David. He will reign over the house of Jacob forever, and of his kingdom there will be no end." (1:32-33 NRSV)

When Mary asks how this is possible, Gabriel makes three further assertions. The first assertion concerns Jesus' conception, which will be by the Holy Spirit, so that the son himself will be holy (1:35). The second assertion concerns Elizabeth's pregnancy, connecting these two conceptions and, curiously enough, confirming this preposterous declaration about Mary's pregnancy with yet another preposterous declaration about Elizabeth (1:36). Then Gabriel comes to his final assertion (translated now somewhat literally): "Because every deed will not be impossible with God." Mary responds, "Behold the slave of the Lord. Let it be with me according to your word."

What Luke does *not* say about Mary here is revealing. In at least two ways, Luke might have amplified his treatment of Mary. First, he might

13. On the interpretation of "favored one," see the helpful observations of Reginald H. Fuller, "A Note on Luke 1:28 and 38," in *The New Testament Age: Essays in Honor of Bo Reicke*, 2 vols., ed. William C. Weinrich (Macon, Ga.: Mercer University Press, 1984), 2:200-6.

have depicted her as a person of honorable status. The brevity of Mary's introduction has already been noted earlier. Luke explains only that she lives in Nazareth (an insignificant place), that she is a virgin engaged to (but not yet able to claim the status of) a descendant of David by the name of Joseph. None of the information that ascribes honor to Elizabeth and Zechariah similarly informs us about Mary's standing as an honorable person. As a priest, Zechariah is identified with the center of the Jewish world, the temple in Jerusalem (1:5, 9). Elizabeth celebrates her pregnancy as the occasion of being delivered from disgrace and restored to community (1:25). As Joel Green has put it, Mary "is not introduced in any way that would recommend her to us as particularly noteworthy or deserving of honor. In light of the care with which other characters are introduced and portrayed as women and men of status in Luke 1–2, this is remarkable."[14]

When Mary identifies herself as "slave of the Lord," however, she does take on a status indicator, one that is both higher than any other she might have and subversive of the very notion of status. In the Greco-Roman world, the status of a slave depended on the status of the slave's owner; the householder determined the status of all those within the household. By claiming for herself the title "slave of the Lord," Mary claims that her honor derives from God, not from any of the normal indicators of status that operated in the first-century Mediterranean world. The one who previously ranked low on any scale of status (whether that of age, family heritage, gender) is the one whom God favors; she is the one whose status derives from her obedience to God.[15]

This feature of the passage will reappear numerous times in Luke's two volumes, for Luke often narrates episodes that involve a shift in the character's identification. For example, in Luke 13, the character who enters the story identified as "a woman with a spirit that had crippled her for eighteen years" exits as "a daughter of Abraham." Zacchaeus appears at the outset of chapter 19 as "a chief tax collector" and "rich," but he emerges from Jesus' visitation as "a son of Abraham." Pivotal to the first

14. Joel Green, "The Social Status of Mary in Luke, 1,5–2,52: A Plea for Methodological Integration," *Biblica* 73 (1992): 457-71 (quotation on 465). Green's article builds upon the earlier work of B. J. Malina and J. H. Neyrey, "Honor and Shame in Luke-Acts: Pivotal Values of the Mediterranean World," in *The Social World of Luke-Acts: Models for Interpretation,* ed. J. H. Neyrey (Peabody, Mass.: Hendrickson, 1991), pp. 25-65.

15. Green, "Social Status," p. 468; Dale B. Martin, *Slavery as Salvation: The Metaphor of Slavery in Pauline Christianity* (New Haven: Yale University Press), pp. 1-49.

account of Saul's conversion in Acts 9 is the identification of Saul initially as the church's persecutor (9:1-2; see also 8:3) and then, following the christophany on the road to Damascus, as its proclaimer (9:19b-22). In the same episode, the exchange in that story between Ananias and the Lord turns on the question of how Saul should properly be identified. Ananias objects to his instructions to go to Paul, insisting that Ananias knows "this man" who has done "much evil . . . to your saints in Jerusalem." And the divine voice responds with a new identification: "Go, for he is an instrument whom I have chosen" (Acts 9:15). Luke understands that God, who is maker of heaven and earth, is also the bestower of identity. In Luke 1, Mary enters the story with virtually no identification beyond her own name, but she leaves identified as a slave of the Lord.

The second way in which Luke might have amplified his treatment of Mary is by characterizing her as the proper Roman matron, a figure who frequently appears in literature contemporary with Luke. For example, Luke is sometimes compared with Dionysius of Halicarnassus, whose extensive *Roman Antiquities* began to appear late in the first century B.C.E. The *Antiquities,* as the title indicates, focus on the origins of Rome and its emergence as a power, with primary attention to rulers, their battles, and their successes and failures. Occasionally, however, Dionysius does venture into elements of cultural history by commenting on religious practices, agriculture, and plagues, most often with a view to celebrating the outstanding character and accomplishments of Rome and its people. Students of Luke take up the *Antiquities* because the speeches contained therein have certain formal parallels to those in Acts.[16]

In Dionysius's history, women figure almost entirely as the property of males, either as wives or as daughters.[17] The overwhelming majority of

---

16. See, for example, Eckhard Plümacher, "The Mission Speeches in Acts and Dionysius of Halicarnassus," in *Jesus and the Heritage of Israel: Luke's Narrative Claim upon Israel's Legacy,* ed. David P. Moessner (Philadelphia: Trinity Press International), pp. 251-66; David Balch, "ἀκριβῶς . . . γράφαι (Luke 1:3): To Write the *Full* History of God's Receiving All Nations," in *Jesus and the Heritage of Israel,* pp. 229-50.

17. This in itself distinguishes Dionysius's story from that of Luke. A comparison of the Lukan portraits of female characters with those found in Dionysius and other Hellenistic historians has not yet made its way into the extensive discussion of women in Luke-Acts. See especially Turid Karlsen Seim, *The Double Message: Patterns of Gender in Luke-Acts* (Nashville: Abingdon, 1994); Ivoni Richter Reimer, *Women in the Acts of the Apostles,* trans. Linda M. Maloney (Minneapolis: Fortress, 1995).

references to women are brief reports, in which no speech is attributed to them and they engage in no independent action. There are occasional exceptions, however. We hear at length from the noble Veturia, mother of Marcius Coriolanus, a woman who plays the role of the Roman matron *par excellence*. Veturia first defends to other women her son's anger against the Romans who exiled him. Later, in an extended speech, she persuades her son to be reconciled with his country and its citizens. Veturia argues that even the anger of the gods can be appeased, so that Marcius' anger should be moderated accordingly. Then she asks Marcius either to comply with her wish or to commit matricide. Finally she pulls out all the rhetorical stops in a lengthy recital of her labor on his behalf. As a widow, she claims:

> "[I was] not only a mother to you, but also a father, a nurse, a sister, and everything that is dearest. When you reached manhood and it was in my power to be freed from these cares by marrying again, to rear other children, and lay up many hopes to support me in my old age, I would not do so, but remained at the same hearth and put up with the same kind of life, placing all my pleasures and all my advantages in you alone. Of these you have disappointed me, partly against your will and partly of your own accord, and have made me the most wretched of all mothers." (8.51.4)[18]

Jewish literature contains its own versions of the revered matron. Second Maccabees celebrates the martyrdom of the mother of the seven martyred brothers:

> Although she saw her seven sons perish within a single day, she bore it with good courage because of her hope in the Lord. She encouraged each of them in the language of their ancestors. Filled with a noble spirit, she reinforced her woman's reasoning with a man's courage. (2 Macc. 7:20-21)

The author of 4 Maccabees, a work roughly contemporaneous with Luke, constructs of this same story a vast encomium to the mother's greatness.

It seems to me reasonable to imagine that Luke *could* have presented Mary in a manner that resembled Veturia or the mother of the Jewish

18. The translation is that of Ernest Carey in the Loeb Classical Library (7 vols.) (Cambridge, Mass.: Harvard University Press, 1945).

martyrs. Luke's storytelling vocabulary, after all, is extensive. He knows how to tell a story in the style of the Septuagint, as he does to great effect in the infancy narrative of Luke 1–2. He can render a speech in a way that befits an ancient historian. He is familiar with the literary convention of the storm at sea and the shipwreck, and he deploys it with style in Acts 27. Certainly he knows the figure of the honorable matron who is celebrated for her strength and her reason (a virtue customarily associated with men). Yet Luke does not borrow from that vocabulary in his treatment of Mary. Not only does he withhold any celebration of the virtues qualifying her as the Messiah's Mother, he also offers no details about her accomplishments in child rearing, no accounting of her sacrifices for her child, no praise of her restraint in grief at Jesus' death. Luke identifies his two volumes as "the events that have been fulfilled among us" (1:1), but those events focus on God and God's action through Mary's son on behalf of Israel and the Gentiles — not Mary herself.

Nothing Will Be Impossible with God

Luke's focus on God's action comes to sharp expression in the final exchange between Mary and Gabriel. Those who are interested in Mary's role in Luke-Acts have largely investigated her final statement at the Annunciation as evidence of her discipleship in an effort to discern the precise connotation of her declaration, "Behold, the slave of the Lord." There is also a need, however, to examine Mary's statement in close relationship to Gabriel's final words: "Nothing will be impossible with God."

Interestingly enough, Gabriel's closing words have received relatively little study in recent scholarship on Luke. By and large, treatments of this passage attend either to Luke's statements about Jesus' birth and their implications for understanding Lukan Christology, or they attend to the final statement of Mary (her self-identification as *doulē* of the Lord) in relationship to the question of Mary's faith, her consent, her cooperation with God.

When commentators do take up Gabriel's final words, they regularly and rightly associate this statement with Old Testament passages.[19]

---

19. Beyond identifying the statement as an allusion to Genesis 18:14 and possibly other Old Testament passages, the secondary literature has amazingly little to say about

The closest parallel comes in Genesis 18, on the occasion of God's promise of a son to Abraham and Sarah. Listening to this preposterous announcement, Sarah laughs, and the Lord responds, "Why did Sarah laugh, and say, 'Shall I indeed bear a child, now that I am old?' Is anything too wonderful for the Lord?" Not only do the contexts both involve miraculous conceptions, but the wording of the question in the Septuagint is very close to that of Luke 1:37.

Similar statements appear elsewhere in the Old Testament. In response to Moses' incredulity at God's promise to feed Israel in the wilderness, God asks, "Is the Lord's power limited?", a question that recurs in Isaiah 50:2 (and see also 59:1).

In Job's answer to the Lord, he recognizes God's power:

I know that you can do all things,
and that no purpose of yours can be thwarted.
'Who is this that hides counsel without knowledge?'
Therefore I have uttered what I did not understand,
things too wonderful for me, which I did not know. (42:2-3 NRSV)

And Jeremiah prays, "Ah Lord God! It is you who made the heavens and the earth by your great power and by your outstretched arm! Nothing is too hard for you" (32:17). Similarly, Zechariah 8:6 reports, "Thus says the Lord of hosts: Even though it seems impossible to the remnant of this people in these days, should it also seem impossible to me, says the Lord of hosts?"

Gabriel's statement plays on the substance, and in some cases also on the wording, of these passages. That is consistent with much in Luke 1–2 that replays important motifs from the Old Testament. The statement points backward to those prior occasions on which God accomplished the impossible. Yet the statement also points forward. For Luke, this is a claim about the future as well as the past, a promise of God's salvific action for Israel and the Gentiles.

To assert that "nothing will be impossible with God" anticipates two other expressions that run throughout Luke-Acts: "word of God" and "plan of God." "Word of God" is one of several expressions Luke employs

---

this statement. Some commentators do identify the statement as apologetic in that it defends Mary's virginity to Luke's audience (Schuerman 57). Others see it as a call to Mary to faith (Nolland 1:57; quoting Mussner).

frequently for the comprehensive character of the gospel, as in that wicked line at the end of Acts 12, where Luke reports that the enemy King Herod was eaten by worms and died, "but the word of God continued to advance and gain adherents." And "plan of God" *(boulē tou theou)* refers to God as the one whose intention and oversight govern the events that unfold, encompassing both the events of Jesus' own life — especially his death and Resurrection — and the way in which the witness moves throughout the cities of the Mediterranean world, stretching in Acts from the ascension of Jesus to the testimony of Paul in Rome. The word *dei* (it is necessary) further underscores the divine will that stands behind events, as when Peter comments in an early speech in Jerusalem (3:20) that the risen Jesus "must" remain in heaven until the time of restoration, or when Peter announces to the Jerusalem authorities, "We must *(dei)* obey God rather than human authority."

Saying that God has a plan is not enough, however; the plan involves a host of developments that might otherwise appear impossible. A few examples will recall those features of the Lukan story that are "not impossible" for God to accomplish.

To begin with, in the context of 1:37, that which is "not impossible" concerns the miraculous conceptions and births of John the Baptist and Jesus. Beyond the immediate context, however, Luke shows the not-impossibility of Jesus as God's Messiah, the one intended for the salvation of Israel, despite the fact that he does not conform to the expectations of the religious leaders of the day. Jesus himself declares that "What is impossible for mortals is possible for God" (18:27). Jesus' own resurrection Luke presents as God's overturning of human judgment. At Pentecost Peter declares that "you crucified and killed [Jesus] by the hands of those outside the law. But God raised him up, having freed him from death, because it was impossible for him to be held in its power" (Acts 2:23-24 NRSV).

The unfolding of that which is "not impossible" continues in the very witnesses to Jesus' Resurrection. Peter, who is thoroughly discredited by his denial of Jesus during Jesus' arrest, emerges in Acts 1 as the spokesperson for believers and the persuasive witness for Jesus. Luke's sole explanation for this transformation comes when Jesus contrasts Satan's urgent desire to disrupt the disciples with his own prayer for Peter's strength (Luke 22:31). The raging enemy Saul emerges from confrontation with the risen Jesus as the gospel's most prominent advocate.

Perhaps the not-impossibility of God's actions emerges most clearly in the extension of the gospel to those previously on the outside — the Samaritans, the Ethiopian eunuch, and then the Gentiles. The dramatically told story of the conversion of the church to the inclusion of the Gentiles might be understood as a narrativization of the theme of the not-impossibility of God's action. Instructed in a dream to take and eat anything present before him, Peter says something that might well be paraphrased as, "But that's impossible! I don't eat those things!" (Acts 10:14). Sent to Cornelius, again Peter declares that social exchange between Jews and Gentiles is impossible (Acts 10:28). Returning to Jerusalem, Peter finds that the gathered faithful once again tell him this is impossible (Acts 11:1-18). And again he must defend his actions — God's actions.

It seems that everywhere the narrator's announcement that he would narrate "the things that have happened among us" (Luke 1:1) means those things that are impossible and yet that God has brought about.

In much of contemporary North American culture, claims about the power of God often meet with suspicion. So enamored are we with our own autonomy that we resent the very notion that God might intercede in our lives. Here we encounter a vast gap between our view of ourselves and that operative in biblical literature. In order to understand Luke's view, we need to understand the larger context in which Luke makes his claims about the power of God. We tend to think of the horizon of the Lukan story as having to do with God and Israel, or perhaps we extend the horizon to encompass God, Israel, and the Gentiles. Yet that way of putting things is strikingly reductive, as the context in which the Lukan story operates is cosmic. This cosmic context is clear early on, in the Lukan version of the temptation narrative — at the conclusion of which Luke reports that the devil, having tested Jesus, "departed from him until an opportune time" (4:13 NRSV). Judas's betrayal of Jesus begins when, as Luke reports it, "Satan entered Judas" (22:3 NRSV), but Satan demands to "sift" all the disciples (22:31). Acts ascribes the lie of Ananias to Satan's interference (5:3), not to mention the numerous occasions on which witnesses defeat Satan's representatives (especially 13:4-12).[20] It should not be surprising, then, to hear Jesus interpret exorcisms

---

20. On the conflict with Satan, see Susan R. Garrett, *The Demise of the Devil: Magic and the Demonic in Luke's Writings* (Minneapolis: Fortress, 1989).

performed by the seventy as indicative of the fall of Satan from heaven (10:17). The context for that which is not impossible concerns not just God and humanity but God and God's own powerful enemies. The cosmos itself is the context.

Mary as the Mother of Believers

The not-impossibility of God's wondrous deeds has much to do with Mary. That not-impossibility — fulfilling the promises, including the outsider, overcoming the resister, even defeating Satan — is first announced to Mary. It is to Mary that the whole story of Luke-Acts is encapsulated in Gabriel's words: "Nothing will be impossible with God."

In response to that claim, Mary utters her own words: "Behold, the slave of the Lord. Let it be with me according to your word" (Luke 1:38). Unlike her predecessor Sarah, Mary does not laugh. Instead, she praises God in the soaring language of the Magnificat. If she later worries and frets and even doubts (see the end of chapter 2), she reemerges in Acts 1 among the believers gathered in Jerusalem prior to Pentecost.

Yet Mary's words stand over the whole of Luke-Acts as surely as do those of Gabriel. God's salvific intervention in human life generates responses. Mary's consent to God's intervention in her life is one of those responses. Her words, "Behold the slave of the Lord," are echoed in the disciples' action of leaving everything and following Jesus, in the faith of the merchant Lydia and the Philippian jailer, and especially in Paul's address to the Ephesian elders, when he speaks of himself as "bound in the Spirit" (Acts 20:22). And, of course, her consent also finds a negative echo in the rejections of Jesus that begin in response to his first sermon in Nazareth and continue even in response to Paul's proclamation in Rome.

This analysis of Mary's words and their place in Luke-Acts does not yet constitute an argument for identifying Mary as the Mother of Believers. Many Protestant interpreters would grant the accuracy of these exegetical observations but would prefer to identify Mary as an exemplar of obedience or a model of faith. What difference does it make which term is used? What is accomplished by going beyond (and I do think it is beyond) the designation of exemplar to the designation "Mother of Believers"?

In favor of identifying Mary as an example, it must be acknowledged that the language of "Mother of Believers" is not biblical. More substantively, to speak of Mary as an example is less gender-specific, presuming that Mary's example is not restricted to that of women (which has certainly been done in the church's life). Perhaps it could also be said that it is easier to explain what we mean when we say someone is an example than when we use an expression like Mother of Believers.

There are, however, significant problems with speaking of Mary as an example. First, Luke's story does not readily lend itself to the identification of human examples. Although readers may find themselves instructed by the foibles as well as the witness of Peter and Paul, it is dangerous to understand them as examples to be imitated. Instead of looking to them as models, they offer evidence of God's action on behalf of humankind. Second, much of what Mary does is unknown to readers and what is known cannot be imitated; it simply is not possible to imitate her maternity or her response to the shepherds or her interrogation of the young Jesus. Third, identifying Mary as an example lends itself too readily to the sort of Protestant moralizing that reduces biblical texts to their outcomes in human conduct; that is, Mary becomes a tonic to render readers into better people.

What does it mean to say that Mary is the Mother of Believers, especially in the context of the Lukan story? First, it implies that one of the "things that have been accomplished among us," to go back to Luke's opening lines, is the creation of a new household. Just as Mary understands herself as a slave in God's household, believers become part of that same household. The Gospel hints at this with its repeated references to Abraham and his children (see 3:8; 13:16; 19:9; see also 1:55, 73). Those encountered in Jesus' ministry — the healed, the reclaimed — are the ones rightly called Abraham's offspring. In Acts, that relationship comes to expression in the portrait of the Jerusalem community sharing together in worship, instruction, fellowship, and material support. And Luke specifically identifies Mary as part of that Jerusalem community (Acts 1:14).

In addition to the creation of a new household, the name Mother of Believers invites readers to pay close attention to the quality of Mary's own thinking, both about her son and about others in God's household. Here I am borrowing from Sara Ruddick and her suggestive work on "maternal thinking," a phrase that refers to the thoughts, judgments, and emotions that characterize the work of mothering.[21] Not necessarily confined to mothers or even to parents, maternal thinking is concerned with preserving the life of the child, with the child's growth, and with nurturing the child into what Ruddick calls an "acceptable" location in society. Luke's story specifically refers to Mary as pondering events concerning Jesus and to her anguish when she does not know his whereabouts.

A further step is involved, however. The Magnificat takes Mary's "maternal thinking" beyond the life of her own child to encompass the well-being of other children. As Mother of Believers, the Lukan Mary here thinks about — and exults in — not only the child she will bear but also those other children who look to God for deliverance. When Mary glorifies God for God's uplifting of the lowly, feeding the hungry, redeeming Israel, even bringing down the mighty from their thrones — she participates in exactly what Ruddick identifies as maternal thinking. She expresses concern for the protection, the well-being, the good will of God's children; in a sense, rhetorically, she takes them for her own.

This point leads directly to the final, and most important, aspect of Mary's motherhood of believers: we receive Mary's story as our own. The difference between receiving Mary's story and imitating Mary needs to be clarified. Consider the experience many of us have at and after a certain age. We become parents ourselves and find that we use expressions we do not remember learning; we sing lullabies we had forgotten that we ever knew. We pass a mirror and wonder how our mother (or father) came to be in that mirror. We have not in fact imitated our mother; indeed, in some cases we have gone to great lengths to avoid imitating our mother. Instead, we have become the mother; we have taken her in.[22]

What is it of Mary that we take in, provided that the Lukan story

---

21. Sara Ruddick, "Maternal Thinking," in *Mothering: Essays in Feminist Theory*, ed. Joyce Trebilcot (Totowa, N.J.; Rowan and Allanheld, 1983), pp. 213-30; *Maternal Thinking: Toward a Politics of Peace* (Boston: Beacon, 1989). Bonnie J. Miller-McLemore considers the relationship between Ruddick's work and Mary in "'Pondering All These Things': Mary and Motherhood," in *Blessed One: Protestant Perspectives on Mary*, pp. 97-114.

22. Dorothy W. Martyn explores the internalization of the parent in relationship to Pauline anthropology in "A Child and Adam: A Parable of the Two Ages," in *Apocalyptic and the New Testament: Essays in Honor of J. Louis Martyn*, ed. Joel Marcus and Marion L. Soards (Journal for the Study of the New Testament Supplement Series 24; Sheffield: JSOT Press), pp. 316-33, see especially pp. 324-26.

has its way with us? It is, of course, Mary's consent to God's intervention in her life, her exultation in God's redemption, her pondering the meaning of Jesus, and certainly her persevering presence with other believers. We take in her confidence that truly all things are possible with God.

This way of putting things coheres with Luke's larger story, precisely because Luke does not show us human beings setting out to find God — to be better and better disciples — but God reaching for human beings. By identifying Mary as our Mother, we do not so much elevate Mary as recognize in her story the fundamental Lukan claim that nothing will be impossible with God, not even our consent to God's will.

Born of a Woman (Gal. 4:4):
A Theological Meditation

LAWRENCE S. CUNNINGHAM

He who had brought into existence all things was brought into existence in the midst of all things.

Saint Augustine of Hippo

Introduction

The Second Vatican Council's dogmatic constitution on the church admonishes theologians, when discussing the Blessed Virgin Mary, to avoid "all false exaggeration" *(ab omni falsa superlatione)* and equally a "too narrow mentality" *(a nimia mentis angustia)* when considering the special dignity of the Mother of God *(Lumen Gentium* 8.67).[1] That instruction of Vatican II and the more general decision to place the Council's reflections on Mary within the context of its dogmatic constitution on the church was a clear effort to reorient the place of Mary within the larger context of the church's saving mission and to rein in some of the more baroque excesses of Marian piety that developed in earlier centuries.

My intention is to obey that admonition carefully. In fact, the bur-

---

1. All conciliar citations are from *Decrees of the Ecumenical Councils,* 2 vols., ed. Norman Tanner (Washington, D.C.: Georgetown University Press, 1993), with the citation of the place in the text.

den of this paper, as will be made clear, will be to unpack at some leisure one simple Pauline assertion in the New Testament, namely, that the Son of God was "born of a woman" (Gal. 4:4).

My encouragement to look through such a tight focus at one phrase comes from my conviction that there are words and phrases in the Christian theological tradition so "thick" and so fraught with accumulated meaning that we can meditate on them in such depth that they yield, in that profound meditation, a whole range of meanings available to us not only in the words themselves but in the ways in which these words have been received within the Christian community over the past two millennia. Biblical concepts, it could be argued, do not yield themselves to any naked reading free from their use in the two millennia of Christian witness.

Who can look at words like "grace" or "cross" or "disciple" without hearing behind them the attempts over those two millennia to plumb their depths? In fact, such a vocabulary makes up what the Germans call *Urworte,* words from which spring up power, resonance, thickness, and depth — words that will never find their full meaning in terms of a dictionary definition or even a paraphrase. Such words are "classic" because they contain within them a surplus of meaning. Alas, it is also true that these words are so bandied about in vulgar discourse that we often find it difficult to consider fully what these words mean. Many words that are central to the Christian tradition are used with such a wide variety of meanings that it is difficult to "hear" them authentically without a searchingly contemplative eye and an equally contemplative ear.

Let me take as an example a word about Mary that has both the pedigree of antiquity and conciliar canonization: the word *Theotokos* ("God Bearer" — in Latin: *Deipara*). The fifth-century Council of Ephesus put its faith about Mary as the "God Bearer" baldly in its very first canon: "If anyone does not confess that Emmanuel is God in truth and therefore that the holy virgin is not the Mother of God (for she bore in a fleshly way the Word of God become flesh), let him be anathema" (canon #1).

Church history tells rightly that the purpose for adopting the title *Theotokos* was a theological choice made against the suggestion of Nestorius that Mary simply be called the "Christ-Bearer." What was at stake, however, was the person of Christ, and the conciliar Fathers understood clearly that words have consequences. *Pace* Nestorius, Mary did not bring forth a nature; Mary brought forth a person who possessed both a human and divine nature. The term *Theotokos,* in short, was an attempt to do justice to that fundamental "coincidence of opposites" that asserts that Jesus Christ was fully human and fully divine.

The conciliar use of the term *Theotokos,* however, cannot simply be reduced to the adoption of a precise term to ensure orthodoxy by fencing off Nestorian error. Nor is it only an antiquarian assertion born of the long-ago struggles over nature and person. The term, in fact, held within it a whole compressed theology relative to the person of Jesus Christ. As Robert Farrar Capon writes, the term "Mother of God" (or, more properly, "God Bearer") "isn't a definition that gives us answers to our questions; it's a sudden illumination of the fact that in Mary, the images of Son, Word, God, man and womb all come together in a new coincidence of opposites. And if you take that paradoxical picture as a seamless whole, you absolve yourself from having to water down any of the images."[2] In other words, the term *Theotokos* carries with it meanings far more fundamental than a mere answer to Nestorian error.

It is for that reason that I want to take a sustained look at the simple Pauline phrase in Galatians 4:4, "born of a woman," with the hope that together we may get some illumination even if that illumination is not "sudden."

Galatians 4:4-6

We might begin with a fuller reading of the text I wish to investigate:

> But when the fullness *(pleroma)* of time *(chronou)* had come, God sent his Son, born of a woman *(gunaikos),* born under the law, in order to redeem those who were under the law, so that we might receive adoption as children. And because you are children, God has sent the Spirit of his Son into our hearts crying "Abba! Father!"

That text has an echo in Romans 8 in which Paul, reiterating a central theme of his, contrasts the disjunction between those who live in spiritual slavery and those who enjoy the spiritual freedom of those who are

2. Robert Farrar Capon, *The Fingerprints of God* (Grand Rapids: Eerdmans, 2000), p. 101.

adopted children of God: "For you did not receive a spirit of slavery to fall back into fear, but you received a spirit of adoption. When we cry 'Abba! Father!' it is that very Spirit bearing witness that we are children of God and if children, then heirs, heirs of God and joint heirs of Christ" (Rom. 8:15-17a).

The difference between the two texts is this: whereas in Romans Paul speaks of adoption in the broad context of his well-known *sarx/pneuma* antithesis of life in the Spirit and life without the Spirit, in Galatians the context is the broad sweep of salvation history. The sending of the Son did not occur at any old time; it certainly did not occur "once upon a time"; it happened in time that could be measured *(chronos)* and, more precisely, at a proper moment in time. Paul makes his assertion, in short, to locate us not in mythic "once upon a time" but in history.

Let us attend to Paul's assertions in the text of Galatians a bit more closely to plumb their depth.

In the fullness of time. The burden of much of what went before in Galatians was Paul's argument that Abraham was justified before the covenant marked by circumcision was enacted. God made his promises to Abraham's seed (singular: *sperma*) and that seed was Christ. The "fullness of time" demanded a waiting period for this singular descendent of Abraham, while in that period the law served as Israel's disciplinarian.

The "fullness of time" also meant that our salvation did not happen at any odd moment but as part of the unfolding plan of God traceable to a specific people who had a specific history. God's plan found its expression in history — a history initiated with Abraham's call recorded in Genesis 12. This assertion is consistent with the ancient affirmations of the kerygmatic preaching found in the *Acts of the Apostles* where the powerful deeds and redemptive acts of Jesus are set against the story of salvation history (see Acts 2:16ff; 3:13ff; etc.) as they are narrated in the famous intervention of Stephen in Acts 7 and reiterated in the opening verses of the first chapter of the Epistle to the Hebrews, with its clear demarcation between the past *(palai)* of the patriarchs and prophets and these latter *(eskatou)* days of the Son.

God sent his Son. The majority of modern exegetes argue that this assertion does not yield any doctrine of the preexistence of the Word. The question about whether the phrase, in fact, makes a case for preexistence is an argument I do not intend to enter for purposes of this paper, but, so that we have truth in advertising, I would like to stipulate that a case can be made for Paul affirming the doctrine of preexistence in this passage and, further, that there are scholars far more competent in these matters than myself who have made that case with some persuasion.[3] One cogent reason for affirming the doctrine of preexistence in this instance is that it sets the entire passage of Paul into a coherent whole. It makes the passage in question rightly a Christ story in miniature. Because preexistence is implied, the story of Christ overlaps with the Abraham story which marks our history in time (i.e., *chronos*).[4]

Born of a woman. This additional stipulation of Paul would not make much sense at all, since all humans are born of a woman, unless Paul understood Jesus to be someone distinguished from all other humans. In that stipulation, then, we can see (or better: we could argue) both the idea of preexistence, albeit not developed, as well as "a change of status that later theology would call the incarnation."[5] It is, in short, for the momentous character and significance of this person "born of a woman" that the assertion is made.

Born under the law. Paul further specifies this one who is sent from the Father. He is born consequent to the giving of the law at Mount Sinai and, further, under its reality. From that assertion of Paul we can make at least two deductions.

First, the "fullness of time" which Paul spoke of earlier is that period between the giving of the law and its abolition as a consequence of the salvific work of Christ. Christ is located in historical time generally and in the time of the revelation of God to the children of Israel specifically. That seemingly innocuous datum has enormous significance when considered in depth, namely, that the Son of God is inexplicable except against the successive expectation of the children of Israel to see the Anointed One come from its own people.

Second, the Son of God was a human with a specific history and a specific pedigree. Christ was not an angel or a demiurge or a power but a man who came from a woman who was a child of Israel. He was, bluntly, a Jewish male with all that that assertion implies. That some, in fact,

3. Brendan Byrne, "Christ's Pre-Existence in Pauline Soteriology," *Theological Studies* 58, no. 2 (June 1997): 308-30. Byrne's article has an excellent bibliographical survey of the literature.

4. I borrow here from Frank Matera's *New Testament Christology* (Louisville: Westminster/John Knox, 1999), p. 106.

5. Matera, *New Testament Christology,* p. 106.

thought Jesus to be an angelic figure was a notion well enough abroad that the author of the Letter to the Hebrews felt compelled to dispel it in the opening chapter of that letter. The simple phrase "born of a woman" is a source of discomfort to anyone with a penchant for docetism or gnosticism in its many manifestations as, for example, the early patristic tradition (think of the description of pregnancy and childbirth in Tertullian's *De Carne Christi!*) loved to insist.

Again: Born of a Woman

I will take it as a fundamental datum that the Pauline confession that Jesus was "born of a woman" is the base point from which reflection on the more particular assertions made about Mary in the rest of the New Testament rest. It is, of course, not without moment that Paul's assertion is the earliest reference we have to Mary in the canonical Scriptures. In the opening part of Paul's Letter to the Romans Jesus is described "as descended from David according to the flesh" (Rom. 1:3), which is the closest analogue we have to the "born of a woman" statement in Galatians.[6] Both assertions insist on birth and not some sort of trans-material manifestation. That Paul asserts, in Romans 1:3, that Jesus is born according to the flesh *(kata sarka)* and reasserts that he is "born of a woman" in Galatians testifies to his earthly and fleshly reality as well as to the precise condition under which he was born: at a certain time in history, which is described as "under the Law" and according to the line of David.

The contemporary Russian Orthodox theologian, Elisabeth Behr-Sigel, has summarized the importance of this text in Galatians rather well:

> Mary is not a feminine divinity. She is the completely human mother of God who, in order to save humanity not as a *deus ex machina* but from within it, assumes all of humanity. In witness to his full humanity the Son of God and God-man was born of a woman, according to the reciprocity-equality underscored by Paul, in order to end a very in-

---

6. For an exhaustive treatment of the concept of the Davidic line, see John Meier, "From Elijah-like Prophet to Royal Davidic Messiah," in *Jesus: A Colloquium in the Holy Land,* ed. Doris Donnelly (New York: Continuum, 2001), pp. 45-83, and the same author's discussion in *A Marginal Jew: Rethinking the Historial Jesus,* vol. 1 (New York: Doubleday, 1991): 216-19.

volved debate. "However in the Lord, though woman is nothing without man, man is nothing with woman; and though woman came from man, so does every man come from a woman and everything comes from God (I Cor 11:11-12).[7]

What Behr-Sigel writes has behind it a long tradition within the Christian witness to the truth of the Incarnation. When the fifth-century monastic master John Cassian wished to distinguish that plain sense of Scripture which sets out a "simple sequence of a historical exposition which has no hidden meaning" from allegorical or spiritual readings he cites three texts: the *paradosis* concerning the Resurrection of Jesus in 1 Corinthians 15, the *Sh'ma* of Deuteronomy 6:4, and our text from Galatians 4. What Galatians asserts, according to Cassian, is the plain sense, which is understood as coming from what is simply "comprised in the sounds of the words."[8]

Cassian, of course, stipulates something that all of the orthodox theologians before his day, arguing against various strands of docetism or gnosticism, insisted upon. Jesus was born of a woman. He took flesh. Writing more than two centuries earlier than Cassian, Irenaeus cites the same text from Galatians as part of a long catena of texts from both the Gospels and the letters of Paul, "plainly indicating [*pace* the gnostics] one God, who by the prophets makes promise of the Son, and one Jesus Christ Our Lord, who was of the seed of David according to his birth from Mary."[9] Irenaeus will cite the same text in other places as he required a reiteration of his argument for the real fleshliness of Christ: Christ was a true man.[10]

My argument would be that in subsequent assertions made by the New Testament writers about Mary, the fundamental fact of the human-

7. "Mary and Women," in *Discerning the Signs of the Times: The Vision of Elisabeth Behr-Sigel,* ed. M. Plekon et al. (Crestwood, N.Y.: St. Vladimir's Seminary Press, 2001), p. 108.

8. "The Fourteenth Conference: On Spiritual Knowledge," in *John Cassian: The Conferences,* trans. Boniface Ramsey, O.P. (New York: Paulist, 1997), p. 511.

9. *Adversus Haereses* III.15.3. All citations are from the old *Ante-Nicene Fathers,* vol. 1.

10. *Adversus Haereses* III.22.1 and IV. 21.1 Saint Thomas Aquinas in his commentary on Galatians a millennium later sees our text as a refutation of a range of heretics including the Valentinians and Nestorius. See *Super Epistolas S. Pauli Lectura* (Turin: Marietti, 1953), p. 610.

ity of Jesus, guaranteed by his birth from a woman, stands behind those assertions found in the plain text of Galatians. I am not arguing that the other writers knew the Pauline text, but I am arguing that they knew the Pauline datum of Jesus as a true human born of a woman.

When discussing later New Testament assertions, it might be better to speak of later New Testament moments in which the assertion that Jesus was born of a woman stands behind moments in which that fact emerges as part of a kind of stunning paradox. Let me provide just a few of those moments to make my point.

First, we have probably recited the prologue of John's Gospel so frequently that it is easy to forget how powerful a claim John is making. "And the Word became flesh and dwelt [NRSV: "lived" for the Greek literal verb "pitched his tent"] among us" (John 1:14). That particular text was a huge stumbling block to those in the early church — the Gnostics and Docetists of various hues and colors — who could not conceive of a divinity enfleshed. John, however, makes that claim stand as a bedrock claim of orthodox Christian belief.

There is a fine theological precedent for juxtaposing the text of Galatians 4 and the prologue of John's Gospel in order to gain insight into the doctrine of the Incarnation: Saint Augustine does it with some frequency in the opening books of the *De Trinitate.* You will remember that Augustine sets up a seeming paradox or a coincidence of opposites in the early part of his treatise on the Trinity: Christ possessed both the form of God *(forma Dei)* and he was also a slave or servant of God *(servus Dei).* Augustine will use our text from Galatians at least ten times in the *De Trinitate* for the precise reason of demonstrating the coincidence of opposites mentioned above; here is a typical example from Book I (chapter 4.22): "In the form of God *all things were made by Him* (John 1:3); in the form of a servant, he himself was *born of a woman, born under the law* (Gal. 4:4)."[11]

Let us not hasten to focus all of our attention on the incarnational claim of John 1:14 without pausing long enough to remember the parallel that John himself is making: Just as divinity dwelt in a special fashion in the tabernacle (and later the temple) in the mercy seat between the cherubim, so now divinity dwells within the flesh of Jesus Christ. Both

---

11. *Saint Augustine: The Trinity,* trans. Edmund Hill (Brooklyn: New City, 1991), p. 82.

the tabernacle and the Mother of Jesus pertain to the world of facticity and creation. It is only a step from that assertion to ponder the role of Mary who gave flesh to Christ. The pitched tent of John 1:14 has some nexus to the concept of *Theotokos*. It was not uncommon in patristic and especially medieval typological understandings to see the ark of the covenant contained within the Holy of Holies as a *figura* of Christ and, by extension, the Virgin Mary. Indeed, some modern scholars have seen the words of the angel saying to Mary that "the Holy Spirit will come over you and the power of the Most High will overshadow you" (Luke 1:35) as an allusion to the *Shekinah* (the Presence) which hovered over the Ark in the Tabernacle.[12]

However much we might or might not accept such a reading, it is very clear that Catholic piety invokes "Ark of the Covenant" (in, for example, the Litany of Loreto) as one of Mary's honorific titles. By itself the title might seem fanciful, but within the context of a long meditation on the scriptural claims with precise places in the canon, such a title seems less arbitrary and more like a contemplative extension of more apparent scriptural insights.

However we may construe the Johannine and Lukan allusions to the ark of the covenant, one thing seems clear and it is this: when we examine the New Testament closely, there does seem to be some intimate nexus between two assertions, namely, that Jesus was really born of a woman and that in his maternal existence there is an analogy between his life and the presence of divinity not unlike the special presence of the *Shekinah* that dwelt within the precincts of, first, the tabernacle, and then in the Holy of Holies of the temple.

If that is, in fact, the case, then we can move a step closer in linking together the assertion that Jesus was "born of a woman" and the assertion that he came from David's line "according to the flesh." Mary becomes the nexus between the hopes of Israel and its realization in the person of Jesus. That link has been made clear in a recent work by the English theologian, Sarah Boss. She writes:

> Mary is said to be a figure for Israel, in whom the people's salvation is conceived and for whom it is born; and Christian tradition has main-

---

12. Raymond E. Brown's *The Birth of the Messiah* (New York: Doubleday, 1977) has a balanced assessment of these claims.

tained that Israel had longed for generations for this salvation — the coming of the Messiah — and that this wish was fulfilled in Jesus. Moreover, biblical scholars have drawn attention to the fact that the Greek word with which Gabriel greets Mary is *chaire*. . . . This is also the word used by the Septuagint in prophecies addressed to the "Daughters of Zion" which look forward to the salvation of the Jewish People. In this way, Mary is cast as a representative of God's people, in whom their deepest hope is about to be realized.[13]

Extrapolations

It would be a gigantic conceptual reach to argue for the legitimacy of other Marian doctrines — her virgin birth or, even more, her immaculate conception or her bodily assumption into heaven — to say nothing of the extra dogmatic pious beliefs and practices tolerated or even promoted by the Roman Catholic Church (Marian shrines, the rosary, etc.) based on a careful meditation of Galatians 4:4. Nor do I intend to do so in this paper even if it could be done. The development of Marian piety as well as doctrinal formulations is beyond my present scope.[14] Finally, I would not wish to argue that the early text in Galatians is the necessary starting point for any fuller systematic theological reflection on Mary.[15]

What can be argued, it seems to me, is that a deep meditation on the Pauline assertion that Christ was "born of a woman" provides a kind of benchmark test for any sustained dialogue about how theologians should think of Mary in the light of the larger picture of Christian revelation. Such benchmarks tests would have to include the following:

(1) A fuller appreciation of the role of Mary in the Incarnation of Christ, which can be developed both by a look forward to the consider-

13. Sarah Jane Boss, *Empress and Handmaid: On Nature and Gender in the Cult of the Virgin Mary* (London: Cassell, 2000), p. 218.

14. Hilda Graef's *Mary: A History of Doctrine and Devotion* (Westminster, Md.: Christian Classics, 1987) is still serviceable as an overview. On recent popular Roman Catholic devotionalism, see the excellent survey by Sandra Zimdars-Swartz, *Encountering Mary: Visions of Mary from La Salette to Medjugorje* (Princeton: Princeton University Press, 1991).

15. For an overview, see Elizabeth Johnson, "Mary and the Saints," in *Systematic Theology: Roman Catholic Perspectives,* vol. 2, ed. Francis Schüssler Fiorenza and John Galvin (Minneapolis: Fortress, 1991), pp. 145-77.

ations of the early patristic tradition as it continues to ponder the role of Mary in the Incarnation but also by looking back into the Old Testament matrix from which the story of Mary's role in the Incarnation is developed. There are such retrospective glances as we have already indicated. By the second century Justin Martyr in his Apology is completing the Pauline parallel of Adam and Christ by indicating Mary to be the Second Eve. Justin, like the evangelists John and Luke, contextualizes the story of the Christ and his mother against the antecedent story of salvation from Adam forward. Irenaeus saw a parallel between the birth of Adam from the virgin soil and the birth of Christ from the Virgin Mary. By the fourth century other such parallels become common. Gregory of Nyssa, for example, sees nothing strange about understanding the burning bush of Exodus 3 as an anticipation of Christ's virginal birth in his *Vita Moysis.* One could multiply the examples.

(2) By insisting on the human birth of Jesus and locating that birth at a juncture between Old Testament assertions and New Testament meditations we come closer to a kind of biblical reading that avoids the reductionism of simple historical assertion and the tendency to "spiritualize" Jesus as a platonic figure dwelling only in the "faith reaction" of his subsequent followers. Galatians 4:4 read in the matrix of the entire Word of God tethers us both to the reality of the meaning of the Incarnation and to a base point from which we can think about the consequences of such an assertion for Christology in general and meditations on theological anthropology in particular.

What does it mean to say that God became man by being born of a woman who was chosen to be his mother? One thing that it means, to be sure, is that the story of salvation, as the Christian faith understands it, is rooted in an almost outrageous particularity. While there has been some tension between Catholic and Orthodox theology, on the one hand, and Protestant theology, on the other, about whether Mary actively cooperated in her *fiat* or whether she was the passive instrument of God's will (with the emphasis on God's will as opposed to Mary's reaction),[16] the one thing all traditions agree on is that Mary was the *terminus a quo* of the historical event of the Word made flesh. She is the one person chosen from all of humanity that made real the Incarnation. Robert Jenson puts

---

16. See Boss, *Empress and Handmaid,* pp. 74-78 for the range of modern theologians who have discussed this issue.

the matter correctly and unapologetically: "The Son has a mother; there exists a *theotokos*. Mary became pregnant, gestated, and gave birth, and the one whom she gestated and gave birth to was the sole and solitary person of the Son of God."[17] Jenson's assertion was anticipated some centuries earlier in a simple quatrain that Saint John of the Cross wrote for Christmas: "The Virgin/heavy with the Word of God/comes down the road/please give her shelter!"[18]

The subsequent development of thinking about Mary, to say nothing of the efflorescence of Marian devotion, cannot be persuasively adduced as a straight line from the biblical witness. Some recent scholars have speculated on the relationship of devotion of Mary to the implicit and explicit need to put a feminine face on God. That speculation is found across the theological spectrum from Reformed to Orthodox and Catholic thinkers.[19] Others have attempted to shift the meditations on Mary away from traditional themes towards a more liberationist view by a renewed look at the Magnificat.[20] The topic is too complex to be treated here, but it is worthwhile to mention it lest anyone think that this paper has attempted to prove more than it intended to do.

(3) Finally, if we assume a more cosmic view of the saving works of Christ — the view that one finds in the high Christology of texts like the Prologue of John's Gospel and the great hymn of Colossians (1:15-20) — we can add one other note about Mary who is the mother of the Savior, a theme that runs through the Fathers and finds one of its constant expressions in the liturgy of the Eastern Church: that the Incarnation recapitulates the outpouring of creation through the Word. This is the theology of creation/re-creation. That vision has also found a way of underscoring the dignity of Mary. God creates and Christ re-creates. Creation is through

---

17. Robert Jenson, "For Us . . . He Was Made Man" in *Nicene Christianity*, ed. Christopher Seitz (Grand Rapids: Brazos, 2002), p. 83.

18. I have slightly modified the translation in *The Collected Works of Saint John of the Cross*, trans. Kieran Kavanaugh (Washington, D.C.: ICS Publications, 1991), p. 73. The Spanish text reads: *Del Verbo divino/la Virgen prenada/viene decamino//le dais posada.*

19. The range of opinion is explored in Elizabeth Johnson's "Mary and the Female Face of God," *Theological Studies* 50, no. 3 (September 1989): 500-526.

20. Ivone Gebara and Maria Clara Bingemer, "Mary," in *Mysterium Liberationis: Fundamental Concepts of Liberation Theology*, ed. Ignacio Ellacuria and John Sobrino (Maryknoll, N.Y.: Orbis, 1993), pp. 482-96. The article is a résumé of the authors' earlier book *Mary: Mother of God/Mother of the Poor* (Maryknoll, N.Y.: Orbis, 1989).

the Word and re-creation through the *fiat* of Mary. That recapitulation has been wonderfully expressed in a prayer of Saint Anselm of Canterbury, so I will let him express that theme here and, as a conclusion to this paper, allow his prayer to have the final word:

> God is the Father of all created things
> Mary is the mother of all re-created things.
> God is the Father of all that is established
> Mary is the mother of all that is re-established.
>
> For God gave birth to Him by whom all things were made
> And Mary brought forth Him by whom all are saved.
>
> God brought forth Him without whom nothing is
> Mary bore Him without whom nothing is good.
>
> O truly "The Lord is with you"
> To whom the Lord gave Himself,
> That all nature in you might be in Him.[21]

21. *The Prayers and Meditations of Saint Anselm,* trans. Benedicta Ward, SLG (New York: Penguin Viking, 1986), p. 121.

A Space for God

ROBERT W. JENSON

Doubtless the archetypical Marian devotion, in the Western church, is the Ave Maria. The first part is simply biblical and hardly poses any theological task. It is the second part that has the punch: *"Ave Maria, mater dei, ora pro nobis. . . ."* "Hail Mary, Mother of God, pray for us. . . ."

There are two theological questions posed by that address. The one concerns the legitimacy and necessity of invoking Mary's or any other saint's prayer. The other is the question: Why invoke Mary's prayer precisely *as* Mother of God? Is her prayer for us somehow different than the prayer of another saint? In some other way, that is, than that in which each saint is of course a particular person whose intercession will show that? Only the second of these questions is ecumenically interesting or requires any very deep thought and is the question on which I will spend this paper. However, the first also continues to divide Christians and must be dealt with in a preliminary way.

It has long seemed plain to this Protestant that the invocation of saints' prayers must be possible and if possible surely desirable. I certainly can ask a living fellow believer to pray for me. If death severed the fellowship of believers, I could not of course ask a *departed* fellow believer to pray for me. But the New Testament hardly permits us to think that death can sever the fellowship of believers — and the eucharistic prayers also of Protestant bodies explicitly deny that it does. Thus there seems to be no reason why I cannot ask also a departed believer to pray for me. And if I *can* do it, there will certainly be contexts where I *should* do it.

Thus there should be no problem about asking Mary in her capacity as *sancta*, Saint Mary, to pray for us.

Those of the Reformers who thought otherwise needed to produce more stringent arguments than any I am aware of their adducing. Simply saying with Melanchthon that there is no scriptural mandate to address individual saints, will not do. Magisterial Protestant churches live by all kinds of practices, perhaps most notably infant baptism and the authority of the New Testament canon, for which no scriptural mandate exists, and which can be justified only by chains of argument far longer than the one just developed for invoking saints. On infant baptism Luther's final word was simply that this had long been the practice of the church, and that he saw no decisive argument against it. One must wonder why the same cannot be said about invocation of the saints.

As for Mary's being θεοτοκος, *mater dei,* Mother of God, that of course is formal dogma for Catholics, Orthodox, and magisterial Protestants alike, laid down among other places in the decrees of Chalcedon. If one balks at *that,* one is simply a heretic.

So the interesting theological question lies in the *linking* of these two, of the epithet "Mother of God" with the solicitation of Mary's prayer. Why mention *this* title in asking for her prayer? Why not just "Saint Mary, pray for us"? Is the invocation of the Mother of God different in kind from the invocation of other members of the company of heaven? A difference marked by invoking her explicitly *as* "Mother of God"? What exactly is the difference?

There are doubtless many ways of answering that question, of which I will here pursue only one. Most importantly, any complete Mariology, Catholic or Protestant, would have to consider in what sense, if any, she can be said to "mediate" salvation; in this essay I am glad to avoid that — mostly, I think, terminological — knot.

For this essay I will start with a type of icon. These are icons, called as a type the Virgin of the Sign, which show a small figure of Christ in a lozenge so located on an image of Mary as to suggest a window into her body. Some such icons carry a Greek inscription, divided to the two sides of the panel and usually in abbreviation. Unabbreviated, the inscription would be: Ἡ χωρη του αχωριστου.[1] The phrase is virtually untranslat-

---

1. The notion is otherwise found in the liturgical tradition. So Marian icons at a certain place in an Orthodox church are ἡ πλατυτερα, because Mary is "wider than the

able in English, due to a quirk of English derivatives from the usable roots. "The Container of the Uncontainable" is the closest direct translation, but rings somehow wrong, containment in the sense of restriction not being quite the point; nevertheless in the following I will use it. Perhaps the most *accurate* translation is paraphrastic and just so inelegant: "the space embracing that which can be encompassed by no space."

The inscription — in Greek anyway — is precise. Mary's womb *is* of course a space. And if she is the Mother of God, if what was in her womb was God the Son, then indeed her womb is the container of the uncontainable; then it is indeed her womb that provides space in our space for the gestating God the Son.

The theological question about Mary's unique place among the holy ones can thus, I suggest, be pointed to as a question about God's space in our world. For of no other single person can it be said that he or she contains the uncontainable God.

John of Damascus formulated a maxim for all subsequent theology: God is his own space,[2] in himself he is "in" nothing but himself. If he creates a world, God occupies the space that he himself is, and the world is another space. And these do not overlap; there is no space to accommodate mixtures of God and creature or almost-gods or a-little-more-than-creatures.

But then, if God is to *have to do* with his created world and not just coexist with it, and especially if he is also to allow creatures to have to do with him, he needs space *in* his creation from which to be present to other spaces therein and at which to allow creatures to locate him; he needs, if I may put it so, a "pad" in creation, a *pied à terre,* a created space to be his own, besides the uncreated space he himself is. And of course the Scriptures do in fact speak richly and variously of created space that God takes as his own abode in his creation.

In the first instance, God's own space within the space he creates is "heaven." The creation is compendiously "the heavens and the earth." And when the creation is in place, it is from its heaven that God "looks down" on his creatures' doings; and when he comes to us it is the division between

---

heavens." The Loretto Litany makes her the "Ark of the Covenant," a typology often found. And the Akathistos Hymn makes her, among a plethora of acclamations, the "Space of the Spaceless God." I am indebted to Robin Darling Young for calling my attention to these instances.

2. *The Orthodox Faith,* 13.11.

heaven and earth that he "rends." When Solomon considers the implausibility of his prayer that the Lord should inhabit the temple he has built, the miracle is that even heaven cannot properly contain the Lord, much less this one building on earth, but that nevertheless God truly inhabits the first and so may perhaps be petitioned to inhabit the second.[3] Or consider Jacob's vision at Bethel: at that spot on earth there is, he sees, a way opened to heaven, a *ladder* reaching upward from earth, on which creatures, the angels, can go back and forth. "Truly," he says, "this is a gate of heaven."

To be sure, Copernicus creates some problems about the location of heaven. I think I have solved them[4] but have no time here to rehearse my ideas on that score. Here it must suffice to say that the biblical notion of heaven is anyway not dispensable: for God to have a history with us, he must have a place not only in himself but in our world, in our space. And the Bible first calls this place heaven.

But now, when the God of Israel creates, he does not create a "cosmos," an assemblage of spaces that is in itself and as a whole timeless. What the God of Israel creates is a history, a reality with a beginning, an end, and a reconciling course of events from the one to the other. Even the first creation itself, as the Fathers of the church noted with some astonishment, is not accomplished except as the history of six days. If then the God of Israel is to take space among his creatures, his space cannot be just a geometrical space beside others, it must be, as we say, a "historical space," a stretch of time. And so it is not just the heaven generally "up there" that he takes for his own occupation; his heaven is — at least short of the Eschaton — the heaven *of* a certain nation. The Lord has space in his creation in that he dwells among a *people,* who as such take temporal space in creation.

Thus there are members of Israel in heaven with God; heaven is a place for God's people and not just for him. Moses and Elijah accompany Christ when he appears in his heavenly glory; and when the door is opened to John the Seer, there is the whole company of saints assembled. And indeed, in many of the narratives it is not possible to distinguish between heaven as a sheer space up there and God's presence among the people of Israel. So the darkness and light from which the Lord thunders

3. 2 Chronicles 6:18-21.

4. Robert W. Jenson, *Systematic Theology,* 2 vols. (New York: Oxford University Press, 1997), 2:120-24.

at Sinai is at once the place from which thunder of course comes, the heavens, and the mountain around which Israel is encamped. When it is said that he "rides upon the wings of the storm," the wings are at once the flying clouds above and the sculptured wings of the cherubim-throne in the Temple.

It is the space *taken up, defined, by the people of Israel,* which is, with sheer heaven, God's space in this world, his *pied à terre.* This must and does show itself in actual phenomena of Israel's life, to a few of which we now turn. And be assured, we are working back toward Mary.

The phenomena in which God's taking of this people for his place is most blatant are the Tabernacle and its successor the Temple. As recent exegesis has made plain,[5] for the writers of the Pentateuch the creation is not complete until the Tabernacle is assembled. For the creation — as Barth put it — is but the continuing "outer basis" of the covenant, and the covenant, "I shall be their God and they shall be my people," is not actual until there is the Tabernacle, that is, a marked-off space in Israel's midst to which they can come to be coming to him, a "tent of meeting."

According to the Old Testament, the Lord really was *in* there, in the tent of meeting and then in the successor, Jerusalem Temple's Most Holy Place. As sheer architecture, the Jerusalem Temple was on the standard pattern of all ancient temples — and indeed Solomon hired foreign architects to build it. An ancient temple was not a hall for assembly, like a church or synagogue; it was a *chamber* enclosing the presence of the god, elsewhere than in Israel mediated by an image. Not to put too fine a point on it, an ancient temple was a God-box; the people assembled for what we would think of as the liturgical functions *outside* the enclosure, in surrounding porticos or courts. Israel's holy place, whether portable or later fixed, was built on just this pattern.

The difference between Israel's holy enclosures and the run of ancient temples was of course that in the Tent of Meeting and in the Most Holy room of the Jerusalem Temple there was no image of the god, which was the very point of other temples. In the Jerusalem Temple's space for God, as in the enclosure of the Tabernacle, there was nothing divine to be seen except in vision.

Nevertheless, God was in that space. There was a winged throne

---

5. E.g., Gary Anderson, "Biblical Origins and the Problem of the Fall," *Pro Ecclesia* 10, no. 1 (Winter 2001): 18-24.

there and the Lord did ride on it. And there was in the Tabernacle and the Temple's inner enclosure another box, another enclosed space, the Ark of the Covenant. In it again there were no images, as the Philistines who once captured it supposed there must be. But God was *there:* when the Philistines set the Ark by Dagon, the impossibility of worshiping both the Lord and another god overthrew Dagon; when David danced before the Ark in triumphal procession, it was "before the Lord" that he danced.

In speaking of the Lord's presence in the Tabernacle and the Temple, in defined spaces in Israel, it is important to keep the order straight: God takes for himself the space enclosed by the Tabernacle or the Most Holy Place in order to dwell among the *people,* not vice versa. It is the people as a whole who are thereby the "Container of the Uncontainable."

And indeed, since it was a people, a phenomenon of history, that delineated the Lord's created space, such bluntly spatial containers as the Most Holy Place or the Ark could not be the only mode of his presence among them. The Lord's presence in Israel was in a "historical space" — the turn of language is odd but telling — and so had more purely historical modes, locations in the *discourse* by which the historical existence of a nation occurs. Two are most noteworthy: prophecy and Scripture.

A prophet was someone to whom "the Word of the Lord" had "come," so that he or she could speak words that were God's words. This is to be very drastically and bluntly understood. As the Lord says in a famous Isaiah passage, the word that the prophet speaks is a word that creates what it speaks to, that will not return empty, but accomplishes events in the world. That is to say, the word that prophets spoke was God's own word, the very word of Genesis 1.

So you could hear the voice of the Lord in Israel, *and* you could tell where that voice was coming from; it had a *location* within Israel. It was coming from the town square or a Temple court, where a prophet was standing. In prophecy, God took space amidst the people.

A prophet's body, moreover, not only marked the place where God was to be heard, it also marked the place where God might be addressed. For a prophet spoke not only for God to the people, but for the people to God. Indeed, in the case of the archetypical prophet, Moses, this intercessory function dominates the narrative.

Did an Israelite want to approach God? He could visit the Temple, or he could go to that "man of God" over there. In a way, a prophet was a sort of historically functioning, mobile Temple; the building in Jerusalem could not go with the people into exile, but prophets could. Temples, moreover, could not follow one another as master and disciple, could not through history accumulate and interpret the presence of God; but prophets could.

Which brings us to Scripture. At least in Israel's own self-understanding, written Scripture, the tablets of the Ten Words written by the Lord in person, belonged to Israel's foundation from the first; their existence is identical with the existence of the covenant, and they were the most important content of the Ark. It is perhaps not possible to say just when Israel's wider oral tradition of narrative and law began to be written, but also writing did not remove the tradition from being shaped by and shaping Israel's continuing history as the narratives and laws were edited and re-edited, each editing both reflecting and shaping a turn in Israel's history with her Lord.

The character of written documents, however, is that, unlike speech per se, they occupy space. Israel's scrolls are portable like prophets, but unlike prophets have no other body than the word they bring. A book of law or prophecy is the very Word of God taking up space. Thus to this day a Torah-scroll is sacred space in Judaism; and until yesterday a Bible was sacred space in Christian piety. The fundamentalists have, I fear, a point: what they call the "inscripturation" of God's Word is vital to faith; for God the Word wants to take up space in our churches and houses.

I was supposed to write about Mary, and have instead been writing about heaven and Israel. It is time to get back directly to Mary.

It is of course the heart of Christian faith that God's presence in Israel is gathered up and concentrated in Immanuel, God with us, in this one Israelite's presence in Israel: he is in person the Temple's *shekinah,* and the Word spoken by all the prophets, and the Torah. And if that is so, then the space delineated by Israel to accommodate the presence of God is finally reduced and expanded to Mary's womb, the container of Immanuel. We must note the singularity of Mary's dogmatic title: she is not one in a series of God's mothers, she simply is the Mother.

To what did Mary, after all, assent, when she said to Gabriel, *"Fiat mihi,"* "Let it happen to me"? Of course it was her womb that with these words she offered, to be God's space in the world. The whole history of Israel had been God's labor to take Israel as his space in the world. And it was indeed a labor, for Israel by her own account was a resistant people: again and again the Lord's angel announced his advent, begged indeed for space, and again and again Israel's answer was "Let it be, but not yet." Gabriel's mission to Mary was, so to speak, one last try, and this time the response did not temporize.

As the created space for God, Mary is Israel concentrated. Ancient hymns directly apostrophize her as "the Ark of the Covenant," by an analogy so obvious that it is more than an analogy. When God's creating Word came in its own singular identity into the world, Mary brought him forth as though she were all the prophets put together — indeed, "as though" is not a strong enough way to put it. And if Christianity does not quite reverence the Book as Judaism reverences the Torah-scroll, it is perhaps because its role has been preempted by Mary's act as Torah's embodiment.

When we ask Mary to pray for us, why should we do this specifically in her capacity as Mother of God? There are two connected answers.

First. Mary is Israel in one person, as Temple and archprophet and guardian of Torah. To ask her to pray for me is to invoke all God's history with Israel at once, all his place-taking in this people, and all the faithfulness of God to this people, as grounds for his faithfulness to me. It is to have Moses say, "Why should the heathen profane your name, because you leave your people in the lurch? Because you leave Robert Jenson in the lurch?" It is to send Aaron to the Tent of Meeting on my behalf. It is to quote all Scripture's promises about prayer at once, as summed up by Jesus, "Whatever you ask the Father in my name will be done."

"Fiat mihi," Mary said, giving her womb as space for God in this world. After all the Lord's struggle with his beloved Israel, he finally found a place in Israel that unbelief would not destroy like the Temple, or silence like the prophets, or simply lose, like the Book of the Law before Josiah. This place is a person. To ask Mary to pray for us is to meet him there.

Second. From the beginning of creation, heaven is God's space in his creation. As the created space for God, there must be a mysterious sense in which Mary *is* heaven, the container not only of the uncontainable Son, but of all his sisters and brothers, of what Augustine called the *totus Christus,* the whole Christ, Christ with his body. But Mary is a person, not a sheer container. That she contains the whole company of heaven must mean that she personally is their presence. To ask Mary to pray for us is to ask "the whole company of heaven" to pray for us, not this saint or that but all of them together. It is to ask the church triumphant to pray for us.

Interestingly, Luther and Melanchthon were happy to say that the saints as a company pray for us, that the church in heaven prays for the church on earth. To invoke Mary's prayer as the prayer of the *mater dei,* the prayer of the Container of the Uncontainable, is to invoke precisely this prayer. Perhaps, indeed, Mary's prayer, as the prayer of the whole company of heaven, is the one saint's prayer that even those should utter who otherwise accept Melanchthon's argument against invoking saints.

The Presence of Mary
in the Mystery of the Church

DAVID S. YEAGO

I

In this paper, I want to defend two theses which I believe myself to have learned from Pope John Paul II's remarkable encyclical on the Virgin Mary, *Redemptoris Mater*.[1] In that encyclical, the Holy Father has, I believe, brought the ecumenical discussion of Mary to a new level of theological seriousness, articulating with unusual clarity the deep assumptions of what might be called the long tradition of "Marian consciousness" in the church, the awareness of Mary as a singular presence within the mystery of salvation. Moreover, and significantly for Protestants, he has done so primarily by way of meditative exposition of the Bible.

Thus the Pope confronts Protestants in a new way with this old-Christian "Marian consciousness" from which we have become alienated, getting behind standard disputes about particular Marian doctrines and practices to engage us on the ground of Holy Scripture. Such an approach calls for new thinking, new reflection, from the heirs of the Reformation, not simply repetition of old dismissals and recourse to old defenses.

My goal in this paper is to respond to the Pope's encyclical, not to

1. Citations are from *Mary, God's Yes to Man: John Paul's Encyclical Redemptoris Mater,* introduction by Cardinal Joseph Ratzinger, commentary by Hans Urs von Balthasar (San Francisco: Ignatius, 1988). References will be given in parentheses in the text and will refer only to the paragraph numbers of the encyclical, which are common to all editions.

expound it, so I shall summarize his rich teaching on Mary's "motherhood" of the church and of the believer rather baldly and formally in two theses:

(1) Mary is irreducibly *present* within the redemptive relationship of the church and of the believer to Christ, not merely as a symbolic figure but as a particular person; there is no redemptive relationship to Jesus Christ that does not contain within itself a relationship to Mary, though not, of course, the *same* relationship;

(2) Mary is present to the church and to the believer both as the *prototype and model* of the church and the believer, and also as an *active agent* of the formation of the church and the believer.

I want to argue that these two theses are in fact well grounded in Scripture and conform to the analogy of the faith, and should be accepted as such by Protestants. Whether the interpretation of Mary's motherhood that I will present in the course of making that case would be acceptable to Roman Catholic (or Orthodox) Christians more generally is beyond the scope of this paper — and it is not, in any case, my question to answer.

Furthermore, I shall deliberately exclude any discussion of the implications of Mary's motherhood thus described for the disputed doctrines of the Immaculate Conception and the Assumption, though the Pope does make connections between Mary's motherhood and those doctrines. One of the conditions under which our wayfaring theology must proceed in this present age is that unlike God, we mortals cannot utter in a single word all that needs to be said. Therefore there are always important matters that must be deferred to another occasion, or perhaps to the Kingdom.

II

Is it true, as the Pope suggests, that Mary is irreducibly present within the redemptive relationship of the church and of the believer to Christ? I believe that this claim *is* true, and that its truth can be seen more clearly if we make the thesis slightly more precise: Mary is irreducibly present in the relationship of the church and of the believer to *the Christ who is at-*

tested in Holy Scripture, the one whom I will call the "scriptural Christ."[2] Since, moreover, it is the scriptural Christ — and he alone — who is the Savior, it is precisely within the *redemptive* relationship to Christ that Mary is irreducibly present. To clarify this claim, some discussion is necessary of what is meant by "the scriptural Christ."

In what is probably the very oldest extant Christian text, Paul's First Letter to the Thessalonians, we are confronted rather abruptly with the claim that what the apostles preach is "not a human word" but "the word of God" (2:13). This claim locates the apostolic preaching in a very specific way within the narrative of the ways of the God of Israel with his people and his creation.

This God, the Holy One of Israel, is the One who creates by speaking and then speaks to what he has created. His word is thus a mighty word, inseparable from his deeds: his words act and his deeds speak. But at the same time, this God knows how to make his very own mighty word audible to creatures within the space and time that they inhabit. He speaks his very own word in the particular human words of his messengers, so that their words, once spoken, do not die away into silence, but as Paul suggests, continue indefinitely to be "at work" mightily among those who receive them in faith. Therefore the testimonies of the God of Israel give life to the soul and make wise the simple; they give joy to the heart and light to the eyes.

In these last days, moreover, this God has at once acted and spoken by a man who *is* his word, his very own co-essential Word, uttered in flesh, in a particular human life. This man, in the singular course of life that he pursues and in the singular fate that he encounters, in his living, dying, and rising again, *is* God's conclusive, unsurpassable word of power and wisdom in which revelation and redemption, truth and life, are given as one in inexhaustible plenitude (cf. 1 Cor. 1:23-24).

This man Jesus, God's word uttered conclusively in flesh, has been raised up from death and sits at God's right hand as Lord and Messiah.

2. I adapt the phrase from John Behr's invaluable *The Way to Nicaea* (Crestwood, N.Y.: St. Vladimir's Seminary Press, 2001), though I am using it with reference to the Christian canon of Scripture as a whole while he uses it with a primary reference to the Old Testament. This bending of the terminology does not indicate any disagreement at all with the material point Behr is making by *his* use of the term. My debt to Behr's discussion of the relationship between Christ and Scripture in the early Fathers is significant throughout this section.

He is not a dead person, one who cannot speak for himself, one of the silent who can only be the passive object of our historical research; he lives and shares in God's own boundless freedom. As the risen and exalted Word, he is competent to provide for his own utterance, when and as he pleases. As a living and free person, he has taken the initiative to make himself known, by commissioning messengers, apostles, and pouring out upon them the Holy Spirit, so that they may proclaim him throughout the world until the end of the age. The apostolic witness is therefore the word of the exalted Word, the testimony through which Jesus Christ, who is himself the conclusive and unsurpassable utterance of God's own powerful Word, presents himself to the nations as their Savior and Judge.

The present age having outlasted the earthly lives of the apostles, the communities they gathered must carry on the apostolic mission, living under the rule of the apostolic testimony and bringing that testimony before the nations until the consummation of all things. It is thus part of the Spirit's provision for the apostolic mission that the church has received a body of New Testament Scripture, a manifold documentation of the apostolic witness. This apostolic Scripture is configured with the Scriptures of Israel around the Word made flesh in a kind of two-syllable utterance of "the one word of God which we have to hear and which we have to trust and obey in life and in death: Jesus Christ as he is attested for us in Holy Scripture"[3] — the scriptural Christ.

It is in the context of such assumptions as these that the Christian tradition, from 1 Thessalonians onward, has never allowed for any *space,* so to speak, between the "real" Christ and the scriptural witness, as though the Scriptures might be only obscure hints and clues to the identity of someone who stands apart from the Scriptures, perhaps even in opposition to them.[4] That possibility, indeed, confronted the church al-

---

3. *The Theological Declaration of Barmen,* Article I.

4. Western mainline Christians today are tempted to be overly impressed by the statistically insignificant dissent from this consensus on the part of a small number of culturally elite European and North American Christians during the past two and a half centuries — a valid if one-sided description of what those of us who belong to such elites call "modern theology" and tend in our culture- and class-centeredness to regard as normative for the present and determinative for the future. Without denying the importance and insights of "modern theology," as far as *this* dissent is concerned we may legitimately recall Augustine's riposte to the Donatists: *Securus judicat orbis terrarum* ("The judgment of the whole Christian world stands firm").

ready in the second century in the complex phenomenon we call "Gnosticism," and its rejection was constitutive for that network of Christian communities which were then beginning to call themselves collectively "the universal assembly," the "catholic church." The Savior to whom the catholic church cries out and bears witness is the *scriptural* Christ, the Word made flesh whom the Spirit presents to us clothed in the words of the prophets and apostles. And this gives a peculiar quality to the relationship of the catholic church to God in Christ; as John Behr has said, "If God acts through His Word, then that Word needs to be heard, to be read, to be understood — the relationship to God is, in a broad sense, *literary*."[5]

I have spent some time on this point because it is fundamental to the baseline question of Mariology: "Is Mary in any sense a 'presence' within the redemptive relationship of the church and of the believer to Christ?" If we are clear in our minds that Christ the Savior is the *scriptural* Christ, that the redemptive relationship of the church and of the believer to *this* Christ is therefore "in a broad sense, *literary*," then the answer to this question is obviously "Yes." *Mary is present within the redemptive relationship of the church and of the believer to Christ by virtue of her presence in the scriptural testimony to Christ.*

The scriptural Christ, "Jesus Christ as he is attested for us in Holy Scripture," is set forth to us, especially in the four Gospels, as one who is surrounded, despite his singularity and in a certain sense his loneliness, by a constellation of *others:* disciples, onlookers, and enemies. Among these "others" is inescapably his Mother, whose narrated relationship to him does not quite fit into any broader category but has its own unique contours. A Christ who did not stand in this singular relationship to Mary would not be the scriptural Christ; when we approach the scriptural Christ we also find with him, in her own place and in her own role, Mary his Mother.

This would be true in a certain sense even if the scriptural testimony never spoke explicitly of Mary, never named her or brought her, so to speak, on stage. The scriptural witness presents Jesus Christ to us as a true

5. Behr, *The Way to Nicaea,* p. 15. For an account of this "literariness" as the sacramental medium of the Spirit's witness to Christ in the church, see my essay, "The Spirit, the Scriptures, and the Church: Biblical Inspiration and Interpretation Revisited," in *Knowing the Triune God: The Work of the Spirit in the Practices of the Church,* ed. James J. Buckley and David S. Yeago (Grand Rapids: Eerdmans, 2001), pp. 49-93.

human being, one like us in all points except sin. Therefore, even if Mary were never mentioned in Holy Scripture, it would nonetheless be an article of the Christian faith that there was indeed a *Theotokos,* a woman who gave human birth to God the co-essential Son of God, a woman rightly called *dei genetrix,* "Mother of God."

But of course this is *not* where Scripture leaves it. The Mother of Jesus is not simply present in the scriptural witness by implication, as a Christological postulate; she is named and presented to us directly as a character in the Christological narrative of salvation. Especially in the Gospels according to Luke and John, moreover, she is sketched in two very different ways not only as a *person* in the story, but, so to speak, as a personage, a figure with a singular role to play, a character whose appearance on the stage is a matter of significant moment. About the *nature* of her role and her presence we will speak in a moment, but it is important first simply to register the *fact* of her presence as a theologically significant personage.

It is here, I believe, that we touch the root of what I have called the ancient "Marian consciousness" of the church, the awareness of Mary as a singular presence within the mystery of salvation. *The church's awareness of Mary as a presence in the mystery of salvation arises from the church's confession that the real and only Savior is the scriptural Christ,* "Jesus Christ as he is attested for us in Holy Scripture." A Christ without Mary, a Christ in whose presence Mary is not also present, would be some other Christ than the scriptural Christ, the construct of some variety of "*gnosis* falsely so-called."[6]

This line of reflection suggests rather alarming conclusions about the meaning of Protestant estrangement from the "Marian consciousness" of the ancient church, and these conclusions need to be faced. I believe that we should take seriously the criticism that the exclusion of Mary from the Protestant consciousness is indeed the symptom of a Christological disease, an alienation from the literary particularity of the scriptural Christ.

The deep root of this alienation lies, I believe, in the dynamics of Christian division. Among Protestants I believe that one outworking of the dynamics of disunity can be seen in a long-standing tension between the scriptural piety that Protestantism sought to inculcate and a persistent

---

6. A phrase used in one of the titles given to St. Irenaeus's great work, more commonly known as "Against Heresies."

worry that the Bible might lead its readers across the boundaries that separate "us" as the true church from "them," the Catholic counterfeit. The scriptural Christ, encountered without rigorous doctrinal-hermeneutical filters, might, after all, turn out to be a lawgiver (as in the Sermon on the Mount), or a promoter of celibacy; and of course, he might also turn out to have a Mother who is more than a postulate of Christological orthodoxy. Has Jesus Christ not indeed tended, in the history of Protestantism, to become at various times and in various ways a rather abstract figure? Even in the older Protestant orthodoxy, was he not at times reduced to a central moving part in a soteriological mechanism, defined by his competence to merit our salvation rather than by the complex detail of the multiple Gospel narratives read in the context of the canon as a whole?

Protestant modernism in some of its moods protested against this theoretically overdetermined doctrinal Christ in the name of the Jesus of the synoptic Gospels, but modernism was likewise unable to grasp the saving particularity of the scriptural Christ. Even more than in Protestant orthodoxy, the Jesus of Protestant modernism is a Savior on a short leash. He must be firmly taken in hand, functionalized within a theory of religion and of our religious need, construed as a signifier transparent to the universal humanistic values he signifies and therefore under their strict control. Otherwise he might lead his followers along strange paths of penitence and apocalyptic expectation, and thereby reduce their economic and moral productivity as citizens of the secular city; he might cruelly demand with all seriousness the death of the sovereign modern self; *he might even turn out to be a Jew.*[7]

The breakdown of denominational identities in the contemporary churches, along with the widespread sense that modernity's rules of the game are losing their obviousness in the culture at large, gives us an opportunity, but no guarantees. We *may* indeed proceed implicitly or explicitly on the "postmodern" premise that every interpretation is a way of seeking power, and therefore harness the figure of Christ ever more arbitrarily and variously to our infinitely diverse felt needs and practical projects; but we may also take the occasion to relearn ancient arts of interpretation that enable an ordered but not finally "scripted" engagement with

---

7. The close connection between anti-Catholicism and anti-Judaism in Neo-Protestantism, and its effect on Neo-Protestant construals of New Testament history and theology, is a phenomenon of crucial significance whose history is yet to be written.

the redemptive particularity of the scriptural Christ.[8] In this latter project, should we choose to undertake it, Mariology has an irreducible place; for the Mother of Jesus is irreducibly and distinctively present within the scriptural testimony to the saving particularity of her son.[9]

III

About the *nature* of that presence, our second thesis makes two claims. Mary is present to the church and to the believer both as the *prototype and model* of the church and the believer, and also as an *active agent* of the formation of the church and the believer. The first claim, that Mary is presented in Scripture as prototype and model of faith and of the church, is less controversial, and is widely granted today among the small number of Protestants who have considered the matter at all. Indeed, the easiest form of Mariological agreement among contemporary Protestants and Catholics is undoubtedly to be found in a shared reading of St. Luke's presentation of Mary as "she who believed" (1:45), the paradigm New Covenant believer who trusts the promise of God and ponders his surprising ways in her heart. Three observations may serve to clarify the implications of this Lukan Mariology.[10]

8. For an attempt at an orientation to these arts, see my aforementioned essay, "The Spirit, the Scriptures, and the Church."

9. This is not to say that Mariology is "necessary to salvation" in the strict sense; the absence of any explicit Mariology from the letters of St. Paul is enough to establish that. But the goal of faith and theology is not to see how *little* of Scripture we can take seriously and still be saved; the goal is the *maximum* of integrity in taking seriously and holding together in our understanding the *whole canon* of testimony with which the church has been provided by the Spirit. After all, the New Testament canon itself is superfluous to what is "necessary to salvation," since the foundational apostolic preaching went on without it. The question of "necessity for salvation" arises when faith and mission have lost their way; it calls us, not to a reductionist purism, but rather to make distinctions *within* the totality of the biblical witness, in order to identify the chief point at which Scripture aims and to trace the ways in which its various aspects hang together to make that point. Since the Spirit's gifts are not given for no reason, we may assume that faith and mission are best served precisely by such disciplined attention to the *whole* of Scripture, not by a strategy of reduction.

10. I regret that limitations of space preclude any account of the two closely connected scenes in which the Mother of Jesus is presented to us in the Gospel of John. Such an account would, I believe, support the main conclusions of this paper.

1. In Luke's presentation, Mary's bodily motherhood, her pregnancy and birth-giving, are introduced in the context of the angel's greeting which calls forth her *faith*. Mary is not simply a biophysical vessel, an unwitting conduit through which the Son of God descends from heaven, picking up mortal flesh along the way. Her miraculous pregnancy is embedded in a drama, a narrative in which she is not only object but also subject, playing a part that engages her whole person. She is *addressed* by the messenger of God, *promised* that the child to which she shall give birth will be the Son of the Most High.

Mary therefore does not figure in the story of salvation only through the bare fact of her pregnancy; her pregnancy is located within a context of covenant and communion, of God's election and promise, and the faith that these evoke. Her role is therefore defined also by the distinctive way in which she *consents* to God's redemptive design, and to her vocation within that design. As Pope John Paul II has written, "The words 'Behold, I am the handmaid of the Lord' express the fact that from the outset she accepted and understood her own motherhood as a *total gift of self*, a gift of her person to the service of the saving plans of the Most High" (par. 39). Her bodily "motherhood" is constituted in the covenant-exchange of divine word and answering faith, a faith that indeed involves "a total gift of self," and therefore, in Pauline terms, the presentation *also of her body* as "a living sacrifice, holy and acceptable to God" (Rom. 12:1).

This sense that Mary's role of giving human birth to the Son of God is embedded in a drama of vocation in which her faith plays a significant part is another of the most elementary perceptions of the Mariological tradition, expressed concisely in the saying of St. Augustine that Mary conceived Christ in her mind by faith before she conceived him bodily in her womb. But the same point was also fully acknowledged by no less than Martin Luther:

> Because Mary the Virgin conceived and gave birth to Christ, therefore Christ was a real, bodily visible human being, and not only a spiritual reality — yet she conceived him and bore him spiritually. How so? Thus: she believed the word of the angel, that she was to become pregnant and give birth. With that very faith in the angel's word, she conceived and gave birth to Christ in her heart spiritually, at the same time that she conceived and gave birth to him in a bodily way. For if she had not conceived Christ spiritually in her heart, she would never have con-

ceived him bodily. . . . Now what did she receive into her heart? Nothing but the word of the angel, that she was to become pregnant with the Son of God. Because she embraced the word and became pregnant with it in her heart, therefore she also became pregnant bodily with that which the word promised her in her heart.[11]

This intertwining of Mary's bodily pregnancy with issues of election, promise, and faith precludes the possibility of viewing Mary as merely the logically necessary presupposition of the Word's true enfleshment. While the Lukan portrayal of Mary is undoubtedly *Christocentric*, she is not reduced to a function in a Christological scheme. Mary is presented as a character with her own profile, one who is confronted with the advent of the Messiah in a singular way and responds to it with words and actions distinctive to her. And the gospel is interested in that profile, in those words and actions — not, to be sure, in competition with its interest in her Son, or simply parallel to it, but precisely as Mary *through* her distinctive words and actions stands *in a specific relationship* to her Son.

Even after the birth of Jesus, moreover, in the story of his presentation in Temple, Mary is mysteriously acknowledged in the Lukan account as having a *continuing* role in the story of salvation. According to Simeon's prophetic testimony, the coming of Messiah will cause division in Israel and provoke enmity; and it is somehow Mary's part to endure this division and enmity as a sword piercing her own being (Luke 2:34-35). There is surely a suggestion here that Mary's role in the story has not ended with parturition; she continues to be linked to her son's coming into the world and to its outcome.

2. As the one addressed in this singular way by the election and promise of God, Mary is not simply a private person but a *public* one; she is called by the angel's proclamation to an *office,* a public role within the communion of God's people and the history of God's salvation. Though the office of the woman who gave birth to God is necessarily unique, it is not without analogy to other roles and offices encountered in the narrative of salvation. The Lukan story of the Annunciation is notoriously constructed out of intricately interwoven reminiscences of and allusions

---

11. *WA* 23:185. This and the other statements of Luther concerning Mary cited in this paper are handily collected in Walter Tappolet, ed., *Das Marienlob der Reformatoren* (Tübingen: Katzmann Verlag, 1962).

to the Scriptures of Israel; like early Christians generally, the Evangelist turns to the Old Testament as the prophetic and typological explication of the new thing that the God of Israel has done in these last days.

Without attempting to untangle all the strands in Luke's web, it can surely be said that one analogy is crucial to the portrayal of Mary's role: the analogy to *prophecy.* While the Annunciation narrative is clearly reminiscent of the several Old Testament stories in which a child is promised to a woman who could not, in the ordinary course of things, bear children,[12] the Evangelist has also woven into his account elements that belong more characteristically to the call-narratives of the prophets.

It is striking, for example, that neither Sarah nor the mother of Samson nor Hannah nor Elizabeth is *addressed* as Mary is addressed. The three men as whom the Lord appeared at the oaks of Mamre announce the promise only to Abraham, while Sarah overhears, just as Gabriel speaks to Zechariah and not to Elizabeth; the angel does speak to the wife of Manoah, but only in the most abrupt and businesslike fashion, without greeting or title; Hannah hears Eli's blessing — "The God of Israel grant the petition you have made to him" — but no direct "word of the Lord." But direct address *is* characteristic of the calling of prophets: Moses and Jeremiah, Ezekiel, Amos, and Jonah, are all spoken to directly, summoned to God's service.[13] Like Mary, moreover, Moses and Jeremiah are bewildered, unable to see how their task can be carried out; to them as to Mary the Lord or his messenger responds with assurance that God's own power will trump the weakness or the incapacity of his servant.

Furthermore, while the angel's reassurance that "Nothing will be impossible with God" (Luke 1:37) directly recalls the Lord's response to Sarah's laughter in Genesis 18:14, neither Sarah nor the wife of Manoah nor Hannah nor Elizabeth is promised the Spirit. However, the Spirit *is* associated with prophecy, as we have just been reminded in the announcement of John's birth: "even before his birth, he will be filled with the Holy Spirit," and like Elijah, he will speak and act under the impulsion of the Spirit (Luke 1:15-17). There is a parallel here between John and Mary, between the child promised in the first scene and the one to whom

12. Cf. Genesis 18:1-15 (Sarah); Judges 13:2-24 (the unnamed wife of Manoah, mother of Samson); 1 Samuel 1:1–2:11 (Hannah). To these must of course be added Mary's kinswoman Elizabeth (Luke 1:5-24).

13. Cf. Exodus 3:1–4:17; Jeremiah 1:4-10; Ezekiel 2:1–3:11; Amos 7:14-16; Jonah 1:1-3, 3:1-2.

a child is promised in the second; if the Spirit marks John as a prophetic figure, then the promise of the Spirit to Mary associates her with prophecy also.

The connection between Mary and prophecy is further strengthened by the context: the opening chapters of Luke depict what Robert Jenson has called a "positive epidemic" of prophecy,[14] all configured around Mary and her child. As Jenson puts it: "Mary . . . appears in these chapters as the central figure of a sudden resurgence of Spirit-inflicted prophecy: the prophetic Spirit comes upon Mary and by virtue of the result of this visitation also upon others."[15] Thus when Mary visits her relatives in the hill country, Elizabeth is filled with the Spirit and speaks blessing upon her kinswoman and her child; even the unborn prophet is moved to inarticulate testimony. The Evangelist is at pains, moreover, to associate the prophesying of Elizabeth and the unborn John specifically with *Mary's word,* repeating the point twice; it is "when Elizabeth heard Mary's greeting" (v. 41) that the Spirit fills her and it is "at the sound of her greeting" (v. 44) that the child leaps in Elizabeth's womb.

This is, to be sure, no glorification of Mary in *abstraction* from her Son; it is as "the Mother of my Lord" that Elizabeth greets her. But she is greeted also as the one who *accepted* this vocation by faith in the divine promise: "Blessed is she who believed that there would be a fulfillment of what was spoken to her by the Lord" (vv. 43, 45). Mary provokes prophecy as the one who brings the Messiah, but here as in the Annunciation narrative, her bodily "bearing" of Christ is inseparable from her faith. To bring the Messiah to the world is for her an office, a role bestowed on her by God's election and promise and accepted by faith.

Yet the blessings pronounced on Mary in the story of the Visitation also remind us that her office cannot simply be *identified* with that of a prophet. Though the Annunciation narrative is reminiscent of the call-narratives of the prophets, the angel's greeting to Mary is more akin to the eschatological proclamation to Israel — "Rejoice, Daughter Zion!" (cf. Isa. 54:1; Zeph. 3:14; Zech. 9:9) — than to anything in the prophetic call

14. Cf. Robert W. Jenson, "An Attempt to Think about Mary," *dialog* 31 (Fall 1992): 259-64. I am deeply indebted to this article especially in this section, but also in other ways. It pursues the Christological and Trinitarian implications of the Lukan account much further than I can do here.

15. Jenson, "An Attempt to Think about Mary," p. 261.

stories. Mary's vocation is related to prophecy, but in a way that is distinctively "blessed."

Jenson has identified the point of distinction thus: "[B]y the Spirit's coming upon Mary she does not like other prophets before or around her bring forth a speech; she brings forth a child."[16] Actually, Mary according to Luke *does* bring forth a speech, or rather a song, whose significance we have yet to consider, but Jenson's point is well taken: the office laid on Mary by the angel, to which she consents in faith, is not centrally to speak words but rather to bear a particular child. The analogy thus described seems to cry out for explication in the terms provided by the prologue to John, which is also concerned with the relationship of prophecy to the coming of Christ:

> [T]his child is personally and identically that Word of the Father communicated by every prophet — the same point is, of course, made by the whole rest of Luke. Mary is the prophet who utters forth the eternal Word himself and as such. It is because the Word is personally and completely spoken by Mary's willing gestation and parturition, that suddenly there are again Spirit-driven prophets. We may say: Mary is the *archprophet,* the paradigm and possibility of prophecy.[17]

That is to say, Mary's faithful bearing of the Word incarnate is the Spirit-wrought antitype of which all prophesying in the Old and New Covenants is either the anticipation or the recollection. All prophecy is the secondary and dependent utterance in "many and various ways" (Heb. 1:1) of that same Word which Mary conceived and bore in his own person, at once in her heart and in her body. All other prophecy is therefore possible only by virtue of this "archprophecy"; what Mary brings forth from her womb is the *truth* of all prophecy and her willing bodily utterance of the Word in person is the *form and measure* of every other act of prophesying.

3. Prophecy in the biblical witness is not only an individual but also a communal vocation; this association of Mary with prophecy as its antitype therefore implies a relationship of Mary to Israel and the church. It is surely no accident that both the Gospel of Luke and the Acts of the Apostles begin with the coming of the Holy Spirit, in the Gospel to Mary and

16. Jenson, "An Attempt to Think about Mary," p. 261.
17. Jenson, "An Attempt to Think about Mary," pp. 261-62.

in the Acts to the disciples, in each case provoking an immediate outbreak of prophecy. Indeed, Luke depicts the events of Pentecost as the fulfillment of Joel's prophecy that in the last days Israel will be transformed by the Spirit into a community in which *all* are prophets, young and old, slave and free, male and female. The church, for Luke, *is* that renewed Israel, to which the Gentiles must now be called, an Israel re-formed by the coming of the Messiah albeit amidst conflict and schism which the twofold testimony of Luke leaves unresolved.[18] How is Mary related to this renewal?

Mary does not fulfill her office from outside the community of God's people but from the inside. Mary is an Israelite woman, whose life is depicted by the Evangelist as "deeply enmeshed in the traditions of Israel."[19] She and her husband obediently bring their newborn Son to Jerusalem to do what was commanded in the Torah; they piously make an annual pilgrimage to Jerusalem for the celebration of Passover. Her canticle is saturated with Scripture; like the virtuous woman in Proverbs, she opens her mouth with wisdom, and on her lips is the teaching of *chesed* (Prov. 31:26),[20] the covenant-devotion that responds to the *chesed* of God, the never-ending "mercy" towards Abraham and his descendants that God has "remembered" in the sending of the Messiah.

At the same time, Mary also belongs to the community of Jesus' disciples. If Mary is "she who believed" *par excellence,* then she is the paradigm of those who receive the reign of God drawing near in the Messiah Jesus, for faith is the fundamental mode in which human beings acknowledge and pay homage to God's reign and God's Anointed. Luke is careful moreover to clarify that Mary *persists through time* in this obedience of faith; confronted with the shepherds' report of angelic testimony to her Son, with Simeon's dark words about the sword that will pierce her heart, and with the intimation given in his twelfth year of the all-consuming vo-

---

18. This is not to say that the church is "all Israel"; the church is the messianically renewed *part* of Israel that awaits reconciliation with "Israel after the flesh" in the consummation of all things. I do not, that is, intend to suggest a supersessionist *replacement* of Israel by the church, but rather a schism *within* Israel, to which the church is one party.

19. Luke Timothy Johnson, *The Gospel of Luke* (Collegeville, MN: Liturgical Press, 1991), p. 56.

20. This reading assumes that something more is meant by Proverbs 31:26 than "she teaches her children to be kind," which most commentators seem to prefer. Even in wisdom literature, I have difficulty accepting that "Torah" and *"chesed"* in such close conjunction could have so blandly moralistic a connotation.

cation that will take her Son away to death,[21] she does not turn aside in frustration or fear but holds in memory what she does not understand and ponders it in her heart.

The Second Vatican Council was right therefore to speak of Mary's *pilgrimage* of faith;[22] the Holy Father's description of this pilgrimage is, I believe, true to the Lukan presentation:

> To believe means "to abandon oneself" to the truth of the word of the living God, knowing and humbly recognizing "how unsearchable are his judgments and how *inscrutable his ways*" (Rom. 11:33). Mary, who by the eternal will of the Most High stands, one may say, at the very center of those "inscrutable ways" and "unsearchable judgments" of God, conforms herself to them in the dim light of faith, accepting fully and with a ready heart everything decreed in the divine plan (par 14).

In this posture, Mary stands at the intersection of the Old Covenant and the New. In her, by God's election and grace, the drama of Old Covenant Israel reaches its turning point, and the vocation of the renewed Israel, the Messianic assembly, the Christian church, is prototypically embodied. She is "Daughter Zion" (Zeph. 3:14; Zech. 9:9), Israel called to receive with joy the advent of the Lord her King, the childless woman to whom is promised a vast multitude of children (Isa. 54:1ff.). Precisely as one who *persists* in her consent to God's proclamation and promise through the course of a temporal pilgrimage, she is also the archbeliever and the archprophet of the New Covenant, the one who paradigmatically receives the reign of God by faith and renders it present in power to the world, all the while walking "in the dim light of faith." She thus articulates in her own being the constant *form* of the existence of the people of God at *every* point in the story of salvation: expectant and receptive faith issuing in prophecy, barren incapacity transmuted by God's Spirit into fruitful virginity, lowliness unexpectedly exalted.

It is, of course, in the dying and rising of Jesus Christ that this form is redemptively constituted; it is to his image, not Mary's, that we are to be conformed for our salvation. Mary's paradigmatic role is different in *kind* from that of her Son: she is *not* the Redeemer but the prototype of

---

21. Johnson, *The Gospel of Luke,* pp. 61-62, notes the parallels between this story and the Resurrection narratives.

22. Cf. *Lumen Gentium,* par 58.

the redeemed; she is *not* the one in whom we participate but the paradigm of that participation. Jesus the Messiah in his dying and rising is alone the *forma formans,* the form-giving form, the one in whom all things hang together (Col. 1:17) and around whose crucified and risen person the whole creation is to be blessedly configured. Mary by contrast is the *forma formata,* the form that has received formation, the prototype precisely of those who are *not* the Savior, but cling to him by faith, and on the way of faith's pilgrimage endure the protracted inscription of his image on their being.[23]

As the paradigm of the existence-in-faith of the people of God, Mary is likewise the archprophet and Christ-bearer in whom the *office* of the church as a prophetic community takes prototypical form. The Gospel of Luke begins with promise that the Holy Spirit will come upon Mary and that "the power of the Most High" will overshadow her (Luke 1:35); it ends with the risen Christ promising the disciples the Holy Spirit ("what my Father promised") and enjoining them to wait in the city until they are clothed with "power from on high" (Luke 24:49). The point is reiterated at the beginning of Acts, in a close verbal parallel to the promise made to Mary: "You will receive power *when the Holy Spirit comes upon you,* and you will be my witnesses . . ." (Acts 1:8). As the Spirit came upon Mary so that she bore the Word incarnate, likewise the Spirit comes upon the church so that it brings forth prophetic words of witness; as Mary by the power of the Most High gave birth to the great King whose royal dominion will never cease, likewise the church, clothed in power from on high, is sent forth to proclaim the reign of this King "in Jerusalem, in all Judea and Samaria, and to the ends of the earth" (Acts 1:8).

We should not, however, move so rapidly to the analogy of mission that we ignore Christ's command to the disciples to "wait in the city" (Luke 24:49). It is just in this "waiting" — so antithetical to our contemporary can-do evangelism-ideologies — that the church identifies most

23. This suggests that it is *not* an adequate account of Christ's redemptive work to view him as a sort of productive prototype of our own authentic existence in faith, as many modernist theologies have done. An adequate doctrine of atonement requires recognition that Christ has acted and suffered in our place in such a way that he does and endures *pro nobis* what we could not do or endure for ourselves. Cf. my essay, "Crucified Also for Us under Pontius Pilate: Six Propositions on the Preaching of the Cross," in *Nicene Christianity: The Future for a New Christianity,* ed. Christopher R. Seitz (Grand Rapids: Brazos, 2001), pp. 87-105.

fundamentally with Mary the Virgin Mother, acknowledging its sheer incapacity to be what it is called to be. Like Mary, the church cannot bring Christ into the world by any strength or ingenuity of its own; no more than a virgin can give birth to a child can we who are "fools, and slow of heart to believe" (Luke 24:25) be Christ's witnesses to the ends of the earth. The church's assumption of prophetic office begins therefore not with a "Grow Your Church" seminar, but with the persistent and expectant *prayer* of the community of disciples in the "upper room" (Acts 1:13), surely an allusion to the "upstairs room" (Luke 22:12) in which the Eucharist was instituted.[24] In the midst of this waiting and praying community, St. Luke is careful to tell us (Acts 1:14), stands Mary the Mother of Jesus, in whom both the poverty and the dignity of the church are prototypically embodied.[25]

IV

We are left with one final and thorny matter. Mary, according to our second thesis, is present in the church not only as "the *prototype and model* of the church and the believer," but also as "an *active agent* of the formation of the church and the believer." This is, of course, the point at which awful specters arise unbidden in every Protestant mind, not in every respect without reason. Protestants have been discouraged from any serious con-

---

24. Cf. Johnson, *The Gospel of Luke*, p. 333.

25. Several times in the discussion following the lecture on which this paper is based, the question arose: "Why Mary? Why should she be regarded as the prototype rather than, say Paul?" The answer, I think, has two parts. First, it is Mary's distinctive placement in the gospel narrative that leads to the conclusion that she is the prototype for Paul's faith, not he for hers. It is she for whom the calling to faith and witness was inseparably joined to the task of giving bodily birth to the Son of God. When Paul tells the Galatians that he is "in the pain of childbirth until Christ is born in you" (4:19), it is a bit difficult to regard him as the prototype of *that* stance. Second, the question may betray a need to *derive* Mary from the gospel-message by a chain of necessary inferences, which is of course impossible. Mary is a contingent phenomenon. But if the gospel is true, then *nothing* in the economy of salvation, indeed, nothing in creation or creation itself, is "necessary" in that sense. If the gospel is true, God's love and freedom are prior to all necessity; all that is, and especially the mystery of salvation, is a meaningful concatenation of contingencies rooted in God's free election. Mary, like Israel, like the form of the sacraments, like the make-up of the biblical canon, is simply one more such contingency.

sideration of the idea of Mary's active "motherhood" in the church by Roman Catholic elaboration of that idea with what heirs of the Reformation must regard, even on the most charitable reading, as truly ill-advised terms such as "co-redemption" and "co-mediation." Such language seems to violate clear biblical rules of speech[26] and in any case must surely be a standing invitation to theological and devotional disaster. Nevertheless, I believe that it is possible and necessary to affirm the active agency of Mary in the church without in any way intruding her into the role that is Christ's alone.

We might begin by asking about the relationship of Mary's *mode of presence* in the church to the possibility of her *agency*. If Mary is present to the church by way of the scriptural testimony to Jesus Christ, if her presence is therefore "in a broad sense, *literary*," what sort of present *agency* is conceivable for her? The answer seems clear: as a literary presence, even a literary presence uniquely presented to us in "God-breathed" words (2 Tim. 3:16), she can be an *agent* towards us only if she *speaks* to us, only if we are *addressed* by her word.

Mary's Son, indeed, is God's very own co-essential word made flesh; his whole life is in every aspect of its concrete particularity a word addressed to us. As a character in the narrative testimony to the Word made flesh, Mary is so to speak *taken up into* this "one word of God which we have to hear and which we have to trust and obey in life and in death," and is set before us by God as the prototype of our formation by faith in the incarnate Word. It is only the presence of Mary in the scriptural testimony to the one word that God addresses to us in the concrete particularity of the human career of Jesus Christ that grants her any recognizable presence at all within the redemptive relationship of the church and of the believer to Christ.

But that presence will be an *active* presence, will encompass a con-

---

26. E.g., "There is one God; there is also one mediator between God and humankind, Jesus Christ, himself human, who gave himself a ransom for all" (1 Tim. 2:5-6); putting the "one mediator" alongside the "one God" surely implies exclusivity ("*only* one God," "*only* one mediator") in both cases. Likewise: "[God] is the source of your life in Christ Jesus, who became for us wisdom from God, and righteousness, and sanctification, and redemption, in order that, as it is written, 'Let whoever boasts, boast in the Lord.'" Here too the context requires that the "wisdom" which Jesus Christ has become for us is our *only* wisdom; this exclusivity must then also attach to the "redemption" grouped here with wisdom.

tinuing *agency* of Mary toward the church and the faithful, only if Mary is presented not only as speaking and acting in relation to God, her Son, and others around her in ways that are exemplary *for* us, but likewise as speaking with authority *to* us. Only if she is not only, as it were, *spoken* to us in the word, but also *speaks* a word to us within the word, will it be possible for her to be recognized as an active presence in the continuing life of the church and of the faithful.

As matters actually stand, there *is* a word that Mary speaks *to* us in the scriptural testimony to Christ: she speaks to us in her song, her Magnificat.[27] Though spoken in the context of her meeting with Elizabeth, the Magnificat clearly transcends the specificity of that situation and proclaims the great deeds of God to "all generations." While Mary's archprophecy consists chiefly in willingly bearing and bringing into the world the Word made flesh, here the archprophet herself utters prophecy, explicating for all the world the "great things" the Mighty God has done for her. This song, which is simultaneously thanksgiving and proclamation, is Mary's word spoken to us within the word. Here she is most certainly presented not simply as a model or example but also as a speaker to whom we should pay heed; that is, she is presented as exercising *agency* towards us.

If the Magnificat is the specific scriptural locus of Mary's active agency in the church, what follows concerning the *character* of that agency? Perhaps surprisingly, it is at this point that Martin Luther has a neglected contribution to make to an evangelical Mariology. Not only did Luther affirm Mary's motherhood of the church and every Christian,[28] but in his sermons, especially those for the Feast of the Visitation, he persistently speaks of Mary as a present agent in the church, precisely as *the*

27. The claim that the Magnificat is, in truth, the word which the Mother of God addresses to the church is not, it should be noted, touched *directly* by historical-critical discussions of historicity, authorship, and sources of the text. Only if we had positive knowledge from other sources that Mary's attitude was quite otherwise, would the former claim be threatened directly by historical-critical questioning; short of that, the question "What is Mary's continuing witness to all generations?" is not simply reducible to the question, "What are the facts behind the Visitation narrative?"

28. "Therefore Mary is Christ's Mother, and the Mother of us all, although he alone lies on her lap. . . . If he is ours, then we are to be in his place; where he is, there we also are to be, and everything he has is ours, and therefore his Mother is also our Mother" (*WA* 29: 655-56).

singer of the Magnificat, in terms that do not seem casual even though they are not developed very fully.

Luther's description of Mary's agency has two related dimensions. To begin with, she is the church's teacher of praise and thanksgiving. "She leads the choir, and we should follow her with singing."[29] But this is not simply an exemplary role; Mary not only models thanksgiving but teaches it: "Learn from this professor *(Meisterin)*, if you want to give thanks."[30] Her Magnificat is not only a model thanksgiving, but a liturgical text sung daily in the church, and, Luther says, "it would be good if it were sung twice."[31] Its authority can only be compared with that of the Lord's Prayer: "If you want to pray for all on earth, take the Our Father. Here [in the Magnificat] you have the general thanksgiving for all things, also for your own affairs."[32]

But in the nature of the case, thanksgiving and praise are necessarily *theological* undertakings; or rather, thanksgiving and praise are the root of Christian theology. To thank and praise God is necessarily to *proclaim* his great deeds and in so doing to *interpret* them. Thus Luther also names Mary "our dear professor and teacher" *(unsere liebe Meisterin und Lehrerin),* who teaches us to understand the Old Testament Scriptures as witness to her Son. "This little maid has seen more acutely into the scriptures than all the Jews, and she has connected with all the prophecies and examples which are to be found anywhere in Scripture."[33] Therefore her canticle is the most concentrated and adequate articulation of the very heart of the Christian faith:

> The dear Virgin is occupied with no insignificant thoughts; they come from the first commandment, "You should fear and love God," and she sums up the way God rules in one short text, a joyful song for all the lowly. She is a good painter and singer; she sketches God well and sings of him better than anyone, for she names God the one who helps the lowly and crushes all that is great and proud. This song lacks nothing; it is well sung, and needs only people who can say yes to it and wait. But such people are few.[34]

29. *WA* 27:241.
30. *WA* 29:452.
31. *WA* 34/I:566.
32. *WA* 29:452.
33. *WA* 29:451-52.
34. *WA* 34/I:566.

Understood in these terms, Mary's "motherhood" of the church consists in the speaking of a word for the church and all the faithful to hear. Mary's word in the Magnificat opens the chorus of Christian praise, and provides the church and all the faithful with the essential words for praise. At the same time, her words of praise are necessarily also words of instruction: she teaches us to see in the coming of her Son the mercy and might of the God of Israel. Just as a mother teaches her children by precept and example the ways of the family, and prepares them to live well in the surrounding human community, so Mary teaches the church and all the faithful the ways of God's household and forms them so that they may live well in the environment of his inbreaking reign in Jesus Christ.

It is moreover chiefly through her *word* to us, through the Magnificat, that Mary's prototypical *embodiment* of faith and prophecy become *graciously* formative for us. Through the Magnificat, her paradigmatic faith becomes not so much an example of impossible purity by which we are measured, as an available form of life into which we are invited to enter. To be formed by Mary our Mother means in the first place to stammer and lisp along with her in her song; in so doing we take our stand with her in faith and join with her in prophecy and praise, and it is chiefly in this way that she shapes us as worshipers and servants of the great King whom she has brought forth into the world.

V

Let me close with a few words of counsel in response to a question that is bound to arise: How might contemporary Protestants begin to recover an appropriate awareness of Mary's presence in the mystery of the church? In the spirit of walking before one tries to run, I have only three simple-minded suggestions.

First, celebrate those feasts of Christ in which Mary appears as a significant personage in the story of salvation: in addition to Christmas, the Annunciation, the Visitation, and the Presentation of our Lord in the temple. If these feasts are suppressed, and their Gospel lessons passed over in the liturgical cycle, then Mary's literary presence in the church is effaced and the figure of the scriptural Christ is truncated.

So keep the feasts: celebrate them even when they occur on weekdays and "not enough people will come" (that terrible phrase that perhaps more than anything else discloses our practical godlessness). Pastors, when you preach on these texts do not be afraid to take Mary as seriously as Scripture takes her. Laypeople, celebrate these feasts with prayer and thanksgiving and the reading of Scripture even if your pastor has more important things to do. The Mother of God cannot, to be sure, replace your pastor; but compared with her your pastor is, after all — only a pastor.[35]

Second, sing the Magnificat. Sing it at home, and sing it at Evening Prayer in the congregation. Of course, this advice requires that Evening Prayer actually be *observed* in the congregation. It would not be a bad way to rediscover the Magnificat for the pastor simply to turn up at the church every evening at a stated time to pray and sing Mary's song with anyone who comes, or alone if necessary. On the other hand, the presence of a pastor is not *required* for Evening Prayer; if the pastor is not interested, no one can rightly stop the people of God from praying and singing together nonetheless.

Third, when you sing the Magnificat, do not de-gender it as contemporary liturgical versions often do. To translate *doulē* with "servant" suggests that the Magnificat cannot become the church's song without ceasing to be the song of the particular woman Mary.[36] If anything in this paper is true, this suggestion should be vigorously resisted. The Magnificat is the church's song because it is the song of the specific Jewish woman Mary, whom God's election and promise have set in the midst of the church as the prototype of the church's faith and prophecy — and therefore as the archsinger of the praise of God's mercy in Christ. When we sing the Magnificat, all of us, male and female together, take our stand with Daughter Zion, the Lord's slave-woman, identifying with her, and joining in *her* song, the primal, and in this life unsurpassable, articulation of the joy of the Kingdom.

---

35. Cf. Charles Williams, "A Dialogue on Hierarchy," in *The Image of the City and Other Essays*, ed. Anne Ridler (London: Oxford University Press, 1958), p. 129: "The Mother of God was not an apostle, yet the apostles were — only apostles."

36. Professor Beverly Gaventa, in conversation, argued for "slave" over any form of "servant," on the grounds that the offensiveness of "slave" is essential to the point. It is precisely *as* a "slave" — but the *Lord's* slave — that Mary claims status. See Professor Gaventa's essay in this volume. I agree entirely with this point; at the same time, however, in *liturgical* use it is chiefly the use of a feminine form for *doulē* that reminds the congregation of the particularity of the canticle as Mary's song. I would suggest "slave-woman," but perhaps greater literary creativity could come up with something better.

Mary the Theotokos and the Call to Holiness

KYRIAKI KARIDOYANES FITZGERALD

Introduction

Thank you for inviting me to join you in this very important theological conference. It is truly a privilege to be in the presence of so many Christians, presenters and participants alike, who are committed to discerning the will of God for our times. No doubt, the desire to come together and explore with each other our appreciation of Mary, the Mother of God, is in itself an ecumenical event of some significance.

This type of theological dialogue, which brings together Christians to reflect upon significant issues, is very important. Our historical Christian divisions have frequently led us to emphasize or underemphasize aspects of Christian teachings, often in a polemical spirit. The spirit of the Christian ecumenical movement calls us to look at our differences in a new light and with a new spirit. Through true ecumenical exchange we learn more about the God of love and about ourselves. A welcomed and humbling benefit of genuine inter-Christian dialogue is that it is a process that calls particular attention to our attitudes, both personal and ecclesial, on a number of related and vital theological issues. As our gathering demonstrates, this is true in the case of authentic interchange regarding our understanding of Mary, the Mother of God.[1]

---

1. Among the important essays from Orthodox theologians dealing with Mary the Theotokos, the following should be noted: Kallistos Ware, "The Sanctity and Glory of the

The manner by which we approach the question of the person and vocation of Mary, the Theotokos, is intimately related to our approach to the gospel and the church as well as salvation, eschatology, the communion of the saints, and what it means to be a human person. In our theological reflections already, we have encountered occasions demonstrating in exquisite detail how intimately connected our understanding of the Theotokos is with a number of these central theological concerns. In addition to this, we may also have brought to the surface some of our own fears, both personal and ecclesial, which are related to the veneration of Mary and the saints. Yes, this certainly may make us feel uncomfortable to some degree, but this experience may not be such a bad thing. It is a sign that we are being challenged in a safe setting to reflect more deeply on aspects of the faith.

The purpose of this presentation is briefly to introduce both the significance of Mary the Theotokos in Orthodox thought, and to address in a more specific way some perspectives that relate to the call to holiness. Our hope is that this paper will contribute positively to the rich and fruitful discussions on the identity and vocation of Mary, Mother of God, as well as her relationship to all believers.

Theology, Worship, and Mary the Theotokos

The Orthodox approach to theology is something much more than an academic discipline, valuable as this is. Scholarly study and research, when conducted well, can serve authentic theology, which is ultimately concerned with God and our relationship with him. From this perspective,

---

Mother of God," *The Way* (Supplement 51, Autumn 1984): 79-94; Elizabeth Behr-Sigel, *The Ministry of Women in the Church* (Redondo Beach, Calif.; Oakwood Publications, 1991), pp. 181-216; Vladimir Lossky, "Panagia," in *The Mother of God,* ed. E. L. Mascall (London: Dacre Press, 1949), pp. 24-37, reprinted in *In the Image and Likeness of God* (Crestwood, N.Y.: St. Vladimir's Seminary Press, 1994), pp. 195-210; Georges Florovsky, "The Ever-Virgin Mother of God," in Mascall, *The Mother of God,* pp. 52-63, reprinted in Georges Florovsky, *Creation and Redemption* (Belmont, Mass.: Nordland, 1976), pp. 171-78; Françoise Jeanlin, *The Place of Woman in the Church and the Question of the Ordination of Women* (Katerini, Greece: Tertios Publications, 1988), esp. "The Place of the Mother of God, the Theotokos, in the Orthodox Church in Relation to the Ordination of Women," pp. 133-55.

authentic theology is actually a vehicle for the gospel dynamic that fully expresses the "life in Christ."

Despite the best of our human efforts, no formal study of theology can "define" God or fully contain the mystery that is God. At best, our greatest human works of theological refection can serve as humble pointers in the direction toward the "life in abundance" (John 10:10). Indeed, it is very possible to have projects labeled as "theology" that distract the author and reader from an authentic relationship with God. Sometimes these distractions are relatively minor. At other times, these distractions can point to a reality that interferes with the gospel message, often creating a "false gospel" of their own. Constant vigilance is required in order to discern the potential distractions in theological reflection.

This foundational perspective is still very important within the Orthodox tradition. For the Orthodox, discerning authentic or "healthy" theology is not a mere speculative exercise. It is, rather, a matter of life and death, since theology serves as a vehicle through which the Author of Life makes himself known. This is the experience of the "life in abundance" promised to us by our Lord and is made present to us through the Holy Spirit who abides in the Church. Through our theological reflection, we are concerned with speaking about the living God, in the presence of God. This is done both for the glory of God and the salvation of all. The intimate connection between glorifying God and serving the salvation of all is expressed in the observation of St. Irenaeus of Lyons: "The glory of God is the human person fully live."[2]

The Orthodox also pay special attention to the identity of the theologian. "The theologian is a person of prayer; a person of prayer is a theologian." This adage is attributed to the fourth-century mystic Evagrius of Pontus. The adage reminds us that the true theologian is a person who is in a relationship with God, who has been tested through his or her life and has experienced communion with God. This communion with God is traditionally referred to by the Orthodox as *theosis,* or deification.[3]

Perhaps these observations help us to appreciate the common Or-

---

2. St. Irenaeus, *Against Heresies,* 4:20:6.

3. From this perspective, the theologian is a person of the Church who is truly whole and holy, and has experienced being taken up into the very life of God. The theologian, furthermore, is able to direct others on their path. It is hoped that those of us committed to vocations in theology, and still fall far short of *theosis,* are at least on our way in this arduous journey.

thodox assumption that theology is to be prayed. And that theology is best expressed through doxology. Through true praise one is not only directed to the object of praise, but one also surrenders oneself in the presence of the object of praise. At the same time, how and what we say through our doxology is of vital importance. Through praise and thanksgiving, one does not "define" that which is essentially beyond human understanding. Definitions presume equality, or more accurately, superiority to the subject of our attention. And so, there is an inseparable and living relationship between dogma and devotion in the consciousness of the Church. For the Orthodox, it is impossible to separate theological truth from worship and the Scriptures.[4]

Theology, more than any other modality of expression, is a discipline that is to be prayed and experienced. This is based upon the central principle founded in the life of the undivided Church that "the word of prayer is the word of faith" *(lex orandi est lex credendi).* Our appreciation of Mary, the Theotokos, is rooted in the worshiping life of the Church and is reflected in our own prayer. Bishop Kallistos Ware states that St. Mary "is the living heart of our piety."[5] He also stresses, "our attitude is traditional, doxological and intuitive" regarding the Holy Virgin.[6] "Tradition" here is generally understood as the life of the Holy Spirit in the Church. And the Orthodox affirm that it is through the life of the Church where our relationship with Mary and the saints is lived most fully.

Essential Perspectives on Mary

The Orthodox Church uses a number of significant terms regarding Mary in its conciliar teachings and liturgical life. In the liturgical tradition, Mary is frequently referred to as "our all holy, immaculate, most blessed and glorified Lady, the Mother of God, and ever Virgin Mary." Of the many titles given to Mary, three terms are especially important. I will only briefly reflect upon them here.

4. See Vladimir Lossky, *In the Image and Likeness of God,* pp. 196-97.
5. Kallistos Ware, *The Orthodox Way* (Crestwood, N.Y.: St. Vladimir's Seminary Press), p. 79.
6. Kallistos Ware, *The Orthodox Way,* p. 80.

The first and most important is that she is the "Mother of God" or *Theotokos*. In a formal manner, this title comes to us from the Third Ecumenical Council held at Ephesus in 431. This term is an important consequence of some of the great Christological discussions that characterized this Council and the period prior to it. Here, for the Orthodox, is the key to our understanding of both this important term and the whole understanding of Mary. The honor that is given to Mary is intimately related to her relationship to Christ. The title "Theotokos" was approved at Ephesus in the first place because it helped to affirm the reality of Christ. Mary is honored, therefore, not in isolation but because of her intimate relationship to Christ, the God who became human. Bishop Kallistos stresses that the designation Theotokos "has a precise and basic theological content. It is the safeguard and touchstone of the true faith in the Incarnation, emphasizing as it does that the child whom Mary bore was not a 'mere' man, not a human person, but the divine person of the only-begotten Son of God, 'one of the Holy Trinity,' yet genuinely incarnate."[7] If Christ is *Theanthropos,* the incarnate God, then Mary his mother is *Theotokos.* Her title, "Theotokos," points us to Christ.[8]

In addition to this, the Greek title "Theotokos" also conveys a subtle nuance of meaning that may be overlooked in its usual English translation as "Mother of God." The term not only conveys the idea of divine maternity, but also conveys the sense of "she who contains the divine." This bears witness to the complete *kenosis,* the self-emptying of God in order to become human. It also causes us to pause and reflect upon what this means for humankind.

In the Vespers service for the Feast of the Annunciation, the following hymn seeks to put to words this ineffable mystery:

> The Archangel Gabriel was sent from heaven,
> To bring to the Virgin the glad tidings of her conception.
> Coming to Nazareth and marveling at the miracle,
> He thought within himself:
> How wonderful that He, whom the heavens cannot comprehend,
> Is born of a virgin;
> That He who has heaven for a throne, and earth for a footstool,
> Finds place within a maiden's womb!

7. Kallistos Ware, *The Orthodox Way,* p. 80.
8. See Elizabeth Behr-Sigel, *The Ministry of Women in the Church,* pp. 181-90.

84

That He upon Whom the six-winged Seraphim
And many eyed Cherubim cannot gaze,
Wills to become incarnate of her.
By one single word:
But it is the Word of God!
Yet, why do I stand by and say not to the Virgin:
Rejoice, full of grace, the Lord is with you!
Rejoice, Virgin purest one;
Rejoice, maiden bride!
Rejoice, Mother of Life,
Blessed is the fruit of your womb![9]

Secondly, Mary is also called "Ever-Virgin," *aeiparthenos.* This title was formally used to describe her at the Fifth Ecumenical Council held in Constantinople in 553 and is frequently used in liturgical texts when referring to her. The Orthodox firmly maintain that Mary had no other children after Jesus and view the scriptural examples of Jesus responding to his siblings in terms of his dealing with other close relatives. The Greek word for "brother" *(adelphos),* as in Mark 3:31, during this era also was frequently used in this manner. At the same time, unlike the theological underpinnings of the term Theotokos, we note that the Fifth Ecumenical Council uses the term "Ever-Virgin" in a descriptive manner and attaches no specific doctrinal significance to this word.[10] In a sense, the term is simply a reaffirmation of the reference to the "Virgin Mary" found in the Creed of the Council of Constantinople in 381, often referred to as the Nicene-Constantinopolitan Creed.

The reference to the virginity of Mary should remind us that perhaps more is implied here than whether Mary had children after the birth of Jesus. The Greek word *parthenia,* virginity, much like the term *Theotokos,* points to more in the Greek than the English translation sometimes indicates. Numerous writings of the early desert ascetics reveal to us that the meaning of virginity *(parthenia),* while it certainly includes the keeping of physical chastity, implies something more. This refers to a dynamic process focusing upon purity of heart. Purity of heart may be quickly identified as a kind of unconditional integrity in the presence of the living God. It was the goal of the early ascetics to conquer their selfish

9. Vesper Hymn, Feast of the Annunciation.
10. Kallistos Ware, *The Orthodox Way,* p. 80.

desires and develop a pure heart before God. This is expressed in the words of the Psalm: "Create in me a clean heart, O God, and renew a right spirit within me" (Ps. 50 [51]). The title *aeiparthenos* invites us to reflect deeply upon Mary's inner state of integrity before God.

Thirdly, Mary is also frequently called in liturgical and personal devotions "All-Holy" *(Panagia)* and "immaculate" *(archrantos)*. These titles were never formally expressed in the decision of an Ecumenical Council, yet they are used frequently by the Orthodox in liturgical prayer and in personal piety. It is very easy for someone from outside the Orthodox family to feel uneasy when encountering these words, since only God is "holy." These words could give one pause to wonder if Mary is being worshiped as a divinity in her own right. The Orthodox would firmly reject this conclusion.[11] The Orthodox have always made it clear that there is an important distinction between our worship of God and the honor we give to Mary and the saints. Mary and the other saints are human persons. Worship *(latriea)* belongs to God alone. From the Orthodox point of view, veneration *(proskinisis)* or honor *(timi)* can rightly be offered to those human persons who are close to God. Therefore, we honor and fervently pray to those blessed, faithful departed who are alive in Christ, as our brothers and sisters. When we honor Mary and pray to her, we pray to her both as our Mother and our sister among the saints.

Each of these terms requires thoughtful elaboration, yet each points to the unique vocation of Mary in the history of salvation. The honor given to her is intimately related to her relationship to Christ. As such, each of the terms of honor affirms that she is and always will be "one of us." She is a full member of the human community who fulfilled her particular vocation.

As first among all the saints, she not only is the human bridge between the Old and New Testaments; Mary, as well as all the saints, is alive in Christ now. The Orthodox affirm that through the life of the Church she is close to us and available to us as our helper and intercessor, through the love of the Triune God. Reminding us of the intimate connection between Mary and the whole of salvation history, St. John of Damascus de-

11. For some reflection on the Orthodox response to the Roman Catholic view of the Immaculate Conception, see Kallistos Ware, "The Sanctity and Glory of the Mother of God," pp. 86-92.

clares: "The name of the Theotokos expresses the whole mystery of God's saving dispensation."[12]

These perspectives are reflected in the following hymn from the Liturgy of St. Basil:

> O full of grace, you are the joy of all creation,
> Of the hierarchy of angels and of all the human race,
> Hallowed temple,
> Paradise of the Word,
> The glory of virginity.
> From you, God took flesh and became a little child,
> He, who is from eternity our God.
> Your womb, he took as throne,
> Your body, he made wider than the heavens.
> O full of grace, you are the joy of all creation!
> Glory to You!

Mary and the Call to Holiness

I would like to identify five theological observations about Mary that are important to the Orthodox. And, by looking at Mary, we may also see that these insights can fully apply to our relationship with God in our growth in holiness. We can find the basis for these insights expressed already in the story of the Annunciation of Mary found in the Gospel of Luke.[13] While the scriptural references to Mary are limited, the Orthodox Church has reflected deeply upon them. Mary is seen as the true and faithful servant of God who is blessed because "she heard the word of God and kept it" (Luke 11:28).

Theocentricity

The first observation is centered upon the characteristic of "theocentricity." Mary's life is centered upon God. Let us remember the words

12. St. John of Damascus, *The Orthodox Faith*, 3:12 (94:1029-32).
13. For significant insights into the Feasts of Mary, see Elizabeth Behr-Sigel, *The Ministry of Women in the Church*, pp. 184-203.

of Mary when she says: "My soul magnifies the Lord, and my spirit rejoices in God my savior" (Luke 1:46-47). Mary's initial response to Gabriel's greeting is not a testimony to human self-reliance. She does not use this opportunity to call attention to her own abilities that may have helped her to be true to God through challenging times. These and other similar alternative responses, silly as these may sound, have never been uncommon for human beings back then, throughout history, or today where one finds the selfish affirmation, "It's all about me." Instead, Mary's first reaction is a small but important pointer to her inner life. She affirms her dependence upon God. Her response reminds us of the words of Jesus: "where your treasure is, there will your heart be also" (Luke 12:34).

The first words of Mary's song of praise direct our attention to what was growing in the depths of her heart. She was already enjoying the loving immediacy of God. While all of humankind still suffered with the consequences of the Fall, she exclaims that God abides with us! This type of theocentricity is not an anxious obsession to appease a distant and judgmental God, one who barely hears the cries of his people. Rather, her fiat bears witness to a compassionate and intimate God who stands with the lowly. This is a God who loved us first, and never ceases to love us as his daughters and sons.

Mary's song extols the reign of God that she has accepted freely. The Good News and the inauguration of the reign of God began in a special way *for Mary* in her womb on the day of the Annunciation. This was the same Good News that was proclaimed publicly by her Son over thirty years later, where he declared: "The time is fulfilled, and the reign of God has come near; repent and believe in the good news" (Mark 1:14).

Because of the unique event that took place "in the fullness of time," Mary enjoys an intimacy with God her Savior that will never be duplicated. At the same time, St. Gregory of Nyssa makes an interesting amendment to this affirmation when he speaks of the relationship between Mary and us. He says:

> What came about in bodily form in Mary, the fullness of the godhead shining through Christ in the Blessed Virgin, takes place in a similar way in every soul that has been made pure. The Lord does not come in bodily form, for "we no longer know Christ according to the flesh," but he dwells in us spiritually and the Father takes up his abode with him,

the Gospel tells us. . . . In this way the child Jesus is born to each one of us.[14]

As we have said, the Orthodox see Mary and her dignity always in intimate relationship with Christ and with us. From the day of the angel's message, she points us to Christ. At the same time, her Son's message is still new for us today: "The time is fulfilled, and the reign of God has come near; repent and believe in the Good News" (Mark 1:14). Despite our personal circumstances, we too are invited to reach for the God who loved us first, as did Mary.

St. Gregory of Nyssa also strongly urges us to "look at him." He points to the greater reality that God's infinite love already resides deep within us. He says this:

> For this is the safest way to protect the good things you enjoy: Realize how much your Creator has honored you above all creatures. He did not make the heavens in his image, nor the moon, the sun, the beauty of the stars or anything else that surpasses understanding. You alone are a reflection of eternal beauty, a receptacle of happiness, an image of the true light. And, if you look at him, you will become what he is, imitating him who shines within you, whose glory is reflected in your purity. Nothing in the entire creation can equal your grandeur. All the heavens can fit into the palm of the hand of God. . . . Although he is so great that he can hold all creation in his palm, you can wholly embrace him. He dwells within you.[15]

St. Gregory of Narek, a tenth-century monk, expresses this intimate relationship between each of us and God in the following simple prayer:

> There was a time when I did not exist. And you created me.
> I did not ask you for favor. And you fulfilled it.
> I had not come into light. And you have seen me.
> I had not yet appeared. And you have taken pity on me.
> I had not called upon you. And you have taken care of me.[16]

---

14. St. Gregory of Nyssa, *On Virginity* (46:324, 838).
15. St. Gregory of Nyssa, *On the Song of Songs,* 2.
16. St. Gregory of Narek, *The Lamentations.*

Freedom

The second observation about Mary concerns the reality of human freedom. Mary exercises her free will in responding to the invitation of Gabriel. Let us remember the words of Mary when she says: "Here am I, the servant of the Lord; let it be with me according to your word" (Luke 1:38). In the story of the Annunciation, Mary freely responds to the invitation to share in the coming of the Lord in a very special way. God did not compel her. God did not force her. Mary had the full human freedom to respond.

Mary's response bears witness to her freedom and to what it means to be a human person. Perhaps one of the most important qualities of being human is the capacity for the exercise of freedom. Freedom is a fundamental aspect of human persons endowed with self-consciousness and a conscience. It is certainly one of the most important gifts given to each of us since this is among the qualities that set us apart from other living creatures. It is through the process of freely making choices that we become more fully human. Throughout our lives, God calls us to freely respond to him. He says to each of us: "I have set before you life and death, blessing and cursing; therefore choose life" (Deut. 30:19).

As a conscious being, the human person is never coerced by the God of love to love him or others. Perhaps God could have created human beings to be more like robots or computers. This, however, would negate other important qualities of human personhood that are related to our ability to choose. A robot cannot experience love or freely give love.

St. John Chrysostom reminds us of the importance of our freedom in relationship to God when he says:

> Since God loves human beings and is beneficent, he does what he can so that we may radiate virtue. God wants us to win glory, and because of this he does not draw anyone by force or constraint. Rather, God attracts by persuasion and kindness all those who are willing to respond and so wins them over. . . . God wishes to have no servant who is unwilling or who is forced into his service. God wants all to come of their own free will and choice, and with gratitude to him for this grace.[17]

---

17. St. John Chrysostom, *Homily on the Gospel of John*, 10.

There are two important aspects of freedom here that must be identified. The first is freedom from sin. "Sin" is not a very popular word in many circles today. But "sin" in this case does not have to be defined in terms of the disobeying of abstract, yet judgmental, moralistic rules. On a more profound level, sin is deeply personal because it promotes the distortion of relationships. Sin affects our relationship with our own selves, with others, with creation and God. The Orthodox would say that we were not created by God to sin but to share in his goodness and life. Therefore, sin is profoundly unnatural!

The second aspect of freedom is the freedom to grow in holiness. For us, this is the Lord's call to a new, abundant life. He reminds us of the centrality of this "abundant life" when he says: "I have come that they may have life. Life in abundance" (John 10:10). The invitation of Christ to share in this "abundant life" is a call to move from the dead end of self-centeredness to God-centeredness, from brokenness to wholeness, from isolation to integration, from sinfulness to fruitfulness. Through our free and affirmative response, this invitation becomes the basis for our journey. It is because of this journey that the believer enters more deeply into the "abundant life" offered by God. It is a new life in which the disciple becomes aware of the love of the Father, by means of the saving activity of Christ, through the fellowship of the Holy Spirit. It is a new life through which the love of God is shared in a personal way. It is experienced to the very depths of our being.

God respects our freedom, and an example *par excellence* of this respect is given to us at the Annunciation. When the angel relates God's plan to Mary, he was, in a deep sense, sharing God's hope for the entire cosmos. God took a risk of infinite proportions at that moment, since Mary could have said "No." The angel had to wait for her response. And it is with both wonder and humility that Mary joyfully offers her consent and, by so doing, speaks on behalf of every woman and man who seeks to have God enter their life.

Mary's intentional act of obedience is in contrast to the willful disobedience we see in the story of Adam and Eve. The old Eve refuses to cooperate with the will of God for her life. Instead, in disobedience, she and Adam choose to turn away from God in order to become "gods without God." This alienates them from God's life-giving providence and consequently, from each other. Their action seems to set a pattern for subsequent generations. Rather than growing with God in the garden of perfect possibilities, humanity has been suffering the many consequences of the Fall. Among the worst consequences of the Fall — besides the loss of fellowship with God — are sin, death, and distorted relationships. From this point on, human relationships became distorted. Human beings passed on from one generation to the next the propensity for distorted relationships, which further misdirected us from authentic life with God, each other, and creation.

Mary's representative "Yes" to the angelic invitation puts an end to this tragic cycle. Because of the significance of her free response, she was viewed by the early Fathers of the Church as the "New Eve." This theme can be found in writers such as St. Justin the Martyr, St. Irenaeus of Lyons, and St. Epiphanius of Salamis. It is a theme that would become popular in subsequent teachers of both the East and the West.

St. Irenaeus reflects the tradition when he says:

> Just as Eve, wife of Adam, yes, yet still a virgin became by her disobedience the cause of death for herself and for the whole human race, so Mary, too, betrothed but still a virgin, became through her obedience the cause of salvation for herself and the whole human race . . . and so it was that the knot of Eve's disobedience was loosed by Mary's obedience. For what the virgin Eve bound fast by her refusal to believe, the Virgin Mary unbound by her faith.[18]

Humility

The third observation about Mary concerns the virtue of humility. Mary receives the invitation to share in God's plan with true humility. Let us remember the words of Mary when she says: "For he looked with favor on the lowliness of his servant. Surely, from now on all generations will call me blessed" (Luke 1:48).

Mary presents us with a valuable expression of true humility. For the Orthodox perspective, humility is essential for the proper exercise of freedom. It is through humility that we are free to become our truest selves in relationship with God. From this perspective, humility is both a condition of being and an active discipline.

18. St. Irenaeus, *Against Heresies*, III:22:1 (6:709-712); see also St. Justin the Martyr, *Dialogue with Trypho*, 100 (6:709-712).

Through its Latin roots, "humility" refers to being "of the earth" or "being grounded," so to speak. It is the discipline of being grounded in who we really are as sons and daughters of God. It is the recognition of our truest identity in relationship to our Creator.

Humility is often misunderstood because it is confused with humiliation. But these are two very different phenomena! Humility is the virtue that facilitates our being "right-sized," that is, not too great and not too small in the presence of God, other human persons, and creation. In a sense, we know who we are in relationship to God, and this enables us to deal honestly with others.

True humility is the opposite of the sin of pride. The sin of pride can be described as the selfish desire to become god without God. Pride is a vice that distracts us from our true vocation. It causes us to fall into the delusion that we are the center of the universe. Sadly, if we believe that we are at the center of the universe, then there is no chance for authentic relationship with God, other human persons, creation, or even with our own selves! Whenever we are at the center of our own universe, all other persons, divine and human, essentially become mere objects to be manipulated. And we progressively become more easily distracted as we listen for the voices that feed this delusion.

Humiliation is quite different from humility. Humiliation is a vice typically used as a weapon to control others. It is all too frequently employed in the ice-cold service of pride. Some have referred to the effects of humiliation as "soul murder." Humiliation is an attack upon the identity of the person created in the "image and likeness of God" (Gen. 1:26). Sadly, the virtue of humility and the vice of humiliation are often confused in the minds and hearts of many persons, including persons in leadership, even religious leadership.

Genuine humility, paradoxically, helps us to know ourselves in relationship to God and frees us from false understandings of self. This foundation helps us summon forth the audacity to approach God, as we are redeemed creatures bearing the divine "image and likeness" (Gen. 1:26). Humility provides the healthy soil from which our relationships with God, others, creation, even our own selves, may grow. As this is a living relationship, people are encouraged to constantly examine themselves in the presence of God.

St. Gregory of Nyssa speaks of the importance of truly knowing ourselves when he says:

Our greatest protection is self-knowledge, and the avoidance of the delusion that we are seeing ourselves when we are really looking at something else. This is what happens to those who do not examine themselves: What they see is strength, beauty, reputation, political power, great wealth, pomp, self-importance, bodily stature . . . and they think that this is what they really are. Such persons make very poor guardians of themselves. Because of their absorption in something else, they overlook what is their own and leave it unguarded. How can a person protect what he does not know? The most secure protection for our treasure is to know ourselves: each one of us must know himself as he is so that he may not be unconsciously protecting something else other than himself.[19]

Collaboration with God

The fourth observation about Mary concerns the invitation to be a co-worker with God. Let us remember her words when she says: "For the mighty One has done great things for me, and holy is his name. His mercy is for those who fear him, from generation to generation" (Luke 1:49-50).

Mary provides for us the supreme example of collaboration or *"synergy"* with God. Synergy is a term used by the Orthodox that identifies the active cooperation between God and human persons. St. Paul uses a form of this word in his first letter to the Corinthians, when he says: "For we are co-workers *(synergoi)* with God; you are God's field, God's building" (1 Cor. 3:9). Our relationship with God involves us in the process of divine reconciliation and healing. There is a sense that we are co-workers or collaborators with God in the salvation of the world.

This bold affirmation endures as an important teaching within Orthodox theology. Synergy begins with our personal cooperation with God for the sake of our own salvation, but this is not a private process. We are not saved in isolation. We are also involved with God for the salvation of others and the whole world. This perspective in no way seeks to diminish God as our Savior and as the giver of salvation. But, this perspective recognizes that God does call us to share in the process as his collaborators. Mary provides a very positive example of this collaboration. Speaking of

19. St. Gregory of Nyssa, *On the Song of Songs,* 1.

the collaboration of God and the Theotokos, St. Irenaeus says: "Mary cooperates with the economy."[20]

In his discussion of the Beatitudes, St. Gregory of Nyssa speaks of this collaboration especially with reference to the work of the peacemaker. St. Gregory says the peacemakers are those

> who imitate the love of God for humankind, who reveal in their own lives the characteristics of God's activity. The Lord and giver of good things completely annihilates anything that is without affinity and foreign to goodness. This work he also directs for you. Namely, to cast out hatred and abolish war, to exterminate envy and banish strife, to get rid of hypocrisy, and to extinguish from within resentment of injuries which linger in the heart.[21]

We believe that God is all-powerful and self-sufficient. These are among the most basic characteristics of God. Yet, the story of Mary as well as other stories from the New Testament and the stories of the saints throughout the ages remind us that God calls us to join with him, not only for our own salvation, but also as his partners in the work of salvation of the world.

The fourteenth-century theologian St. Nicholas Cabasilas reflects upon the collaborative work of Mary with God's plan for the salvation of the world when he says:

> The Incarnation was not only the work of the Father and of his Power and his Spirit . . . but it was also the work of the will and faith of the Virgin. Without the consent of the all-pure one and the cooperation of her faith, this plan would have been as unrealizable as it would have been without the intervention of the three Divine Persons themselves. Only after teaching and persuading her does God take her for his Mother and receive from her the flesh that she wills to offer him. Just as he voluntarily became incarnate, so he willed that his mother should bear him freely, with her own full and free consent.[22]

We are reminded of the example of the collaboration of Mary and the other saints at virtually every opportunity for common prayer within

20. St. Irenaeus, *Against Heresies,* 3:21:7.
21. St. Gregory of Nyssa, *On the Beatitudes,* Homily 7.
22. St. Nicholas Cabasilas, *On the Annunciation,* 4-5 (19:2).

the Orthodox Church. This is because human collaboration with God is an important element of the gospel dynamic. In almost every liturgical service we hear the following petition: "Calling to remembrance our all-holy, pure, most blessed and glorified Lady, the Theotokos and Ever-Virgin Mary, together with all of the saints, let us commend ourselves and one another and our whole life unto Christ our God."

God has not given up on inviting us to join with him for the salvation of the world. He calls us today! St. Nicholas Cabasilas writes about this essential quality of the loving God when he says:

> God pours himself out in an ecstasy of love. He does not remain in the Heavens and call to himself the servant he loves. No, he himself descends and searches out for such a servant, and comes near, and lets his love be seen, as he seeks what is like himself. From those who despise him, he does not depart; he shows no anger toward those who defy him, but follows them to their very doors, and endures all things, and even dies, in order to demonstrate his love.
>
> All this is true, but we have not yet declared the highest things of all: for not merely does God enter in close fellowship with his servants and extend to them his hand, but he has given himself wholly to us, so that we become temples of the living God, and our members are the members of Christ. The head of these members is worshipped by the cherubim, and these hands and feet are joined to that heart.[23]

Notice how this reference talks about God's unyielding love. It is a love "to folly." God is not unlike a fool in love with us. He stands by us even as we reject and ignore him, day after day; and even dies to demonstrate this love! St. Nicholas then goes on to tell us there is something else even more wonderful than this. God desires to join with us so that we become his hands and feet, joined to his heart. These vivid and powerful words serve to emphasize the basis of the collaboration to which God calls his sons and daughters.

This passage from Nicholas Cabasilas also gives us insight into Mary's relationship with God. Perhaps it is not unreasonable to say that Mary had been open to the divine love and willingly cooperating with God's love ever since the first moment of her existence. Her invitation to

23. St. Nicholas Cabasilas, *On the Divine Liturgy* 2:132.

become the Mother of God the Word, in a deep sense, was the opportunity for which God was waiting, "in the fullness of time."

As a result of her cooperation with God, St. Epiphanius tells us:

> Mary had been the occasion of life and through her, life had been born in us. It is for this reason that the Son of God has come into the world. "There where sin had abounded, grace had more abounded" (Romans 5:20). . . . When death came, life came and more of it in order that life might come in place of death, chasing death which came to us through a woman. And he came to us precisely through a woman and thus became for us the Life.[24]

Relationship

The fifth and final theological observation I wish to share with you about Mary concerns the value of relationship. Let us remember the words of Mary when she says: "He has helped his servant Israel in remembrance of his mercy, according to the promise he made to our ancestors, to Abraham and to his descendants, forever" (Luke 1:54-55).

Authentic relationship is a consequence of the positive expression of our human freedom. Simply stated, we can either freely choose to love another or turn our gaze away. When we turn towards another in loving relationship, we become caught up in their life to some degree. We also share our life with them. When we freely turn to God in humility, we deepen our relationship with him and we become caught up in the divine activity of salvation.

There is an ancient axiom that states: "A solitary Christian is no Christian." This means that the very definition of Christian implies both a relationship with Christ and a relationship with others who are faithful followers of Christ, both living and departed. When we are united with Christ, we are also united with each other. As Christians, our discipleship is one in which we are not simply guided to the Father through Christ in the Spirit. Our discipleship is such that each of us is "knit together" with everyone else who is in Christ, both living and departed. St. Paul tells us that "we must grow up in every way into him who is the head, into

---

24. St. Epiphanius, *Panarion*, 128 (42:729).

Christ, from whom the whole body, joined and knit together by every ligament with which it is equipped, as each part is working properly, promotes the body's growth in building itself up in love" (Eph. 4:16).

Every one of us is created by the same Triune God. Because of this, there is a foundational relationship among us, which is established in the very structure of creation. According to the Orthodox perspective, we are relational beings from the beginning. We are conciliar persons. We are called to relationship. To be a "person" from this perspective calls us to "face forward." "Facing forward" connotes the essential meaning of the theological Greek word for person, *prosopon.* Perhaps to take it one step further, facing forward compels us to "reach out."

Again, the story of Mary's example is very illuminating. Shortly after the Annunciation, we see Mary seeking out her cousin Elizabeth. Mary could not keep her joy to herself. The experience of God's invitation, the "Good News," had to be shared. Mary "had" to reach out to Elizabeth. And so, we see how the gospel dynamic had already begun to work among God's people.

Whenever we choose to turn away, rather than reach out, we run the risk of becoming "individuals." A number of Orthodox theologians today, including Metropolitan John Zizioulas, Metropolitan Maximos Aghiorgoussis, Bishop Kallistos Ware, and Professor Christos Yanaras, have emphasized the importance of the "person" as distinguished from the "individual." When we speak of the "individual" from this theological perspective, we are usually referring to a human being who is isolated, self-contained, and self-absorbed. A "person," on the other hand, is a unique human being in a growing relationship with others. The Greek word, *prosopon,* means "facing forward." And the Latin word, *persona,* means "sounding through." Both terms, while not identical in connotation, nevertheless imply a dynamic relationship with another reality. Mindful of the Trinitarian relationships, we could say that the human being is truly a person when he or she is open to the other, engaged in a growing relationship, and in communion. We encounter daily countless temptations toward individualism and, hence, isolationism. In the face of this, we must affirm that we become more fully human when we are *persons* in a loving relationship with God and with others.

This loving relationship also includes those cherished ones who have gone before us, the saints, and among them Mary the Theotokos. When we turn our gaze to her image in an icon, we see her most often in the presence of her Son, in some manner directing our attention to Him. We see this, for example, in the popular *"Hodegitria"* icon. The title of this icon may be translated as "she who guides" or "she who directs." Mary is depicted holding the infant Jesus with her left hand. With her right hand, she points to the Lord, as if beckoning us to come to him. Not unlike her initial reaching out to her cousin Elizabeth, she lovingly reaches out to us from paradise now through her intercessory prayer. As followers of the Lord, we are intimately related to him and to one another. This principle of interrelationship is the basis of our prayers to one another and for one another.

Conclusion

The Orthodox Church has a rich understanding of Mary the Theotokos. It is an understanding that is rooted in the witness of Scripture and tradition. It is expressed through the liturgical services of the Church and in the piety of the faithful. In honoring Mary, the Church simply affirms the fact that God first honored her in calling her to be the mother of Jesus Christ. The honor that the Church gives to her recognizes her unique vocation in the divine plan of salvation. At the same time, the honor that we direct to her reminds us that Mary is truly one of us. She is one with us in our humanity and in our discipleship. As such, she provides us with a valuable example of a person of faith. She is truly the one who "heard the word of God and kept it" (Luke 11:28).

Today, radiant, even more joyful and eager than ever, Mary the Theotokos desires to share the Good News about her Son with us. And so, with this in mind, the Church sings to her:

> It is truly fitting to sing your praises, O Theotokos, the ever blessed, pure and Mother of our God. You are more honorable than the cherubim, beyond compare more glorious than the seraphim. In virginity you gave birth to God the Word. Most Holy Theotokos, You do we magnify.[25]

25. Hymn from the Matins Service.

The Blessed Virgin Mary
in Evangelical Perspective

TIMOTHY GEORGE

Last year we installed a new pulpit in the chapel of Beeson Divinity School. It features four carved figures from the history of Christian preaching, one from each of the stated eras of church history: Saint John Chrysostom from the early church, John Hus from the Middle Ages, John Knox representing the Reformation, and George Whitefield, apostle of the Great Awakening. Each is shown holding the Holy Scriptures, signifying the commitment of our school to train ministers of the gospel who are faithful proclaimers of the Word of God. What was the attitude of these four preachers to the Blessed Virgin Mary? Although Chrysostom died several decades before the promulgation of the Marian title Theotokos at the Council of Ephesus in 431, he nonetheless extolled the virgin mother of Jesus. John Hus, too, for all his challenge of ecclesiastical authority, maintained a firm devotion to the mother of Jesus. On the other hand, Knox and Whitefield, sons of the Reformation, reflect the hostility (Knox) and neglect (Whitefield) of Mary typical of evangelical religion, especially in its radical Calvinist and Free Church expressions.

The deep anti-Marianism of Knox is shown by an incident that happened in his early life as a Protestant. Having been delivered from "the puddle of papistry," as he called it, he was taken to be a prisoner in the French galleys where he remained for nineteen months. On one occasion, he tells us, while he was serving in the galleys, the Catholic chaplain of Knox's ship held forth a beautifully painted wooden statue of the Blessed Virgin Mary and encouraged Knox and the other prisoners to genuflect and show proper reverence. When the statue of Mary was forcibly placed in Knox's hand, he grabbed it and immediately threw it overboard into the sea. "Let our Lady now save herself," he said. "She is light enough; let her learn to swim!" Never again, Knox adds, was he forced to commit "idolatry" by kissing and bowing to the image of the virgin Mary.[1]

Although I am a Baptist, not a Presbyterian, I belong to an ecclesial tradition decisively shaped by the likes of Knox. Does evangelicalism have a place for the Blessed Virgin Mary or, like Knox of the galleys, have we thrown her overboard once and for all? Without compromising the Reformation principles of *sola gratia, sola fide,* and *sola scriptura,* can we evangelicals understand and honor Mary in ways, as our conference brochure puts it, "that are Scripturally based, evangelically motivated, liturgically appropriate, and ecumenically sensitive"? This is the dilemma of the two Johns. Can John Knox and John Chrysostom stand side by side with shoulders touching on the same pulpit — to say nothing of John Calvin and John of Damascus?

I am by no means the first theologian within the evangelical family to pose these questions. Back in the 1950s, a spiritual descendent of Knox in Scotland, Principal George A. F. Knight, declared that "it is incumbent upon Protestants to cease to be merely negative to the mother of our Lord."[2] Knight was one of several Protestant biblical scholars who did important exegetical work in placing Mary within the whole scope of biblical revelation, setting forth motifs and ideas that would be echoed in chapter 8 of *Lumen Gentium,* the writings of Cardinal Ratzinger, and the papal encyclical, *Redemptoris Mater.* Still earlier in the twentieth century,

---

1. This anti-Marian antidote, retold with variations in detail, became a staple of Scottish Protestant hagiography. The incident was first described in Knox's *History of the Reformation in Scotland:* "Soon after the arrival at Nantes, their great *Salve* was sung, and a glorious painted Lady was brought in to be kissed and amongst others, was presented to one of the Scottishmen then chained. He gently said, 'Trouble me not; such an idol is a curse; and therefore I will not touch it.' The Patron and the Arguesyn, with two officers, having the chief charge of all such matters, said, 'Thou shalt handle it'; and so they violently thrusted in his face, and put it betwix his hands; who seeing the extremity, took the idol, and advisedly looking about, he cast it in the river, and said, 'Let our lady now save herself: she is light enough; let her learn to swim.'" John Knox's *History of the Reformation in Scotland,* ed. William C. Dickinson (New York: Philosophical Library, 1950), 1:108.

2. George A. F. Knight, "The Protestant World and Mariology," *Scottish Journal of Theology* 19 (1966): 55. This article was based on Knight's earlier contribution, "The Virgin and the Old Testament," *Reformed Theological Review* 12, no. 1 (1956).

A. T. Robertson, a Southern Baptist New Testament scholar of note, published a book titled *The Mother of Jesus* (1925) in which he said: "I have felt for many years that Mary the mother of Jesus has not had fair treatment from either Protestants or Catholics. . . . She is the chief mother of the race, and no one should be allowed to take her crown of glory away from her." If Roman Catholics have deified Mary, Robertson said, evangelicals have subjected her to "cold neglect." We have been afraid to praise and esteem Mary for her full worth, he said, lest we be accused of leanings in sympathy with the Catholics.[3] Robertson is right. It is time for evangelicals to recover a fully biblical appreciation of the Blessed Virgin Mary and her role in the history of salvation, and to do so precisely as evangelicals. We may not be able to recite the rosary or kneel down before statues of Mary, but we need not throw her overboard.

To flesh this out a bit, I want to begin with a brief overview of the evangelical tradition and why I think what I have suggested is in keeping with the best impulses of evangelical theology and piety. Then, I want to look at five motifs within the history of Marian devotion, with special attention to evangelical concerns about each of them. And finally, I will close by offering two poems, one by an Anglican priest, the other by a Welsh Baptist theologian.

The Evangelical Tradition

Who are evangelicals? Evangelicals are a worldwide family of Bible-believing Christians committed to sharing with everyone everywhere the transforming good news of new life in Jesus Christ, an utterly free gift that comes through faith alone in the crucified and risen savior. To put it more simply, evangelicals are gospel people and Bible people. We do not claim to be the only true Christians, but we recognize in one another a living, personal trust in Jesus the Lord, and this is the basis of our fellowship across so many ethnic, cultural, national, and denominational divides.

Seen more broadly, evangelicalism is a renewal movement within historic Christian orthodoxy. Its theology and piety have been enriched by many diverse tributaries, including Puritanism, pietism, and Pentecos-

---

3. A. T. Robertson, *The Mother of Jesus: Her Problems and Her Glory* (New York: George H. Doran, 1925), pp. 11, 20, 16.

talism, but its sense of identity as a distinctive faith community, what we might call the evangelical *tradition,* has been shaped decisively by three major episodes: the Protestant Reformation, the Evangelical Awakening, and the Fundamentalist-Modernist controversy. The reformers of the sixteenth century rediscovered a theology of grace that had been obscured, though not completely lost, in the medieval church. They wanted to reorder the church on the basis of the Holy Scriptures, God's Word written. Though they differed among themselves on many issues, the reformers held fast to what later became known as the material and formal principles of the Reformation: justification by faith alone and the sufficiency of the Bible as the normative rule of belief and practice.

The Evangelical Awakening of the eighteenth century was a great movement of God's Spirit led by John and Charles Wesley, George Whitefield, and Jonathan Edwards among others. Much of what we associate with later evangelicalism comes from this period: hymn singing, mass evangelism, the modern missionary movement, Bible societies, Christian social reform, and so on. All of these were controversial at the time, not unlike today's intra-evangelical debates over worship styles and strategies for church growth.

At the dawn of the twentieth century, the evangelical consensus, shaped by the Reformation and the Awakening, was threatened by theological liberalism and the rise of destructive biblical criticism. This led to fierce debates and church splits between fundamentalist defenders of the faith and their accommodationist critics. After World War II, a new coalition of postfundamentalist evangelicals emerged. These "neo-evangelicals" believed as firmly as the Fundamentalists in the truthfulness of the Bible, but they also believed that Christians should be intellectually strong, culturally literate, socially engaged, and cooperative in spirit.

Blessed with visionary leaders such as Billy Graham, John Stott, Carl F. H. Henry, and Bill Bright, evangelicals in the past half-century have moved from the margins into the mainstream, with a proliferation of publications, institutions, and parachurch ministries. In recent years, evangelicals have begun to recognize the basic continuities that link them with other orthodox Christians on such key doctrines of the faith as the Holy Trinity and the classic Christology of the early church. Fundamentalism ignored this great dogmatic tradition in the name of simple biblicism, while liberalism denied it in the interest of cultural relevance. More and more evangelicals are now reading the church fathers, recovering aspects of liturgical prayer, and finding spiritual wisdom from martyrs and saints hitherto uncelebrated in traditional evangelical piety. Evangelicals are discovering that it is possible to be catholic without being Roman Catholic, and orthodox without being Greek Orthodox, just as one can also be Lutheran without being "Missouri Synod" Lutheran, and even Baptist without being "Southern" Baptist.

Can the evangelical reengagement with the wider Christian tradition include a place for Mary? Put otherwise, without forsaking any of the evangelical essentials, can we echo Elizabeth's acclamation, "Blessed are you among women, and blessed is the fruit of your womb!" (Luke 1:42), or resonate with the Spirit-filled maid of the Magnificat: "My soul magnifies the Lord, and my spirit rejoices in God my Savior, for he has looked on the humble estate of his servant. For behold, from now on, all generations will call me blessed" (Luke 1:46-48)?

Five Marian Motifs

Daughter of Zion

Mary stands, along with John the Baptist, at a unique point of intersection in the biblical narrative, between the Old and the New Covenants. When Mary cradles the baby Jesus in the temple in the presence of Anna and Simeon, we see brought together the advent of the Lord's Messiah, and the long-promised and long-prepared-for "consolation of Israel." The holy family is portrayed as part of a wider community, namely "all those who were looking for the redemption of Jerusalem" (Luke 2:38).

In one sense, Mary appears in the infancy narratives as the culmination of a prophetic lineage of pious mothers — Sarah, Rachel, Hannah, and not forgetting Tamar, Rahab, and Ruth who appear in the Matthean genealogy. All of these are predecessors of Mary. There is a sense in which any one of them could have been the mother of the Messiah. According to one interpretation of Genesis 4:1, when Eve exclaims at the birth of Cain, "I have gotten a man from the Lord," she supposes that this her firstborn son was already the fulfillment of the prophecy of Genesis 3:15, the seed of the woman who would bruise the head of the serpent.[4] It does

---

4. Among others, Luther accepted this interpretation: *LW* 1, 242. For further dis-

not count against this argument that, in divine providence, the mother of the Messiah would eventually turn out to be a virgin. For on the most literalistic reading of the infancy narratives — which evangelicals are happy to accept — that a *virgin* should conceive and bear a Son, and that that Son should be the Messiah, was an enormous surprise, not least to Mary and Joseph! Only in the light of the event did Isaiah 7:14 make sense as a prophecy fulfilled in Christ.

But Mary as the handmaiden *(doulē)* of the Lord, chosen to give birth to the Messiah, is more than the culminating figure among the mothers of Israel. As the Daughter of Zion she is the kairotic representative of the eschatological and redeemed people of God: Israel itself. George Knight and Max Thurian, as well as a number of Catholic exegetes, have developed this kind of Marian typology, pointing to numerous Old Testament texts in which Israel is personified as a woman, notably Isaiah 62:11, "Say to the daughter of Zion, behold, your salvation comes . . ."; and Lamentations 2:13, "O daughter of Jerusalem . . . O virgin daughter of Zion." Included in this catena are also several verses in which the daughter of Zion is depicted as being in the labor of childbirth:

> Writhe and groan, O daughter of Zion, like a woman in travail. (Micah 4:10)

> For I heard a cry as of a woman in travail, anguish as of one bringing forth her first child, the cry of the daughter of Zion gasping for breath. (Jeremiah 4:31)

It is this kind of typological reading that allowed the early church, from Justin Martyr and Irenaeus onward, to depict Mary as the new Eve, the one through whose obedience the disobedience of the first Eve was reversed.[5]

Evangelicals have much to learn from reading Mary against the background of Old Testament foreshadowings. It is popular in some circles for evangelicals to refer to themselves as "New Testament Christians." When it

---

cussion, see Kenneth A. Mathews, *Genesis 1–11:26,* in *The New American Commentary* (Nashville: Broadman and Holman, 1996).

5. See Joseph Ratzinger, *Daughter Zion: Meditations on the Church's Marian Belief* (San Francisco: Ignatius, 1977); Max Thurian, *Mary: Mother of All Christians* (New York: Herder and Herder, 1964).

comes to questions of baptism and church order, the New Testament clearly has a kind of functional priority within the biblical canon, but the term "New Testament Christian" can hardly be purged of its Marcionite connotations. Evangelicals, especially those coming from the Baptist and Anabaptist wings of the movement, need to be reminded that Scripture is indeed one book with a true inherent unity. The image of Mary in the New Testament is inseparable from its Old Testament antecedents, without which we are left with not only a reductionist view of Mary, but also of Christ.

Under the heading of "Mary, the Daughter of Zion," however, there is also a note of dissonance that must be registered from an evangelical perspective. For in the Old Testament, Israel is not only portrayed as a virgin daughter, but also as an unfaithful bride. "'Like a woman unfaithful to her husband, so you have been unfaithful to me, O house of Israel,' declares the Lord" (Jer. 2:20). The waywardness of Israel is contrasted to the covenant fidelity of God: "'Return, faithless people,' declares the Lord, 'for I am your husband. I will choose you . . . and bring you to Zion'" (Jer. 3:14). It is hard to relate this theme to Mary, immaculately conceived and sinless from birth. But there are at least hints in the Gospels of another Mary — "one who does not understand what God's purposes are, who intervenes when she ought to keep silent, who interferes and tries to thwart the purpose of God, who pleads the ties of filial affection when she should learn faith."[6]

We hear echoes of this in the way the Marian irritation-passages are interpreted in the history of the exegesis of the early church. For example, in commenting on Mark 3:31-34 (with its parallel in Matthew 12), where Mary and Jesus' brothers are portrayed as "standing outside" while they send someone else in to call for Jesus, Hilary of Poitiers conflates this text with John 1:11 and says,

> But because he came to his own and his own did not receive him, in his mother and brothers the synagogue and the Jews are prefigured abstaining from going in to and approaching him.[7]

If Hilary is right, Mary is shown here as one who is outside the Messianic community, indeed as one who participates with other members of Jesus'

---

6. David C. Steinmetz, "Mary Reconsidered," in *Memory and Mission: Theological Reflections on the Christian Past* (Nashville: Abingdon, 1988), p. 124.

7. In *Evangelium Matthaei Commentarius* 12.24. Quoted in Stephen Benko, *Protestants, Catholics, and Mary* (Valley Forge, Pa.: Judson, 1968), p. 107.

family in his deliberate rejection! Tertullian offers a similar interpretation in both *De Carne Christi* and *Adversus Marcionem.* Without pressing the image of Mary as the prototype of the synagogue, with its damaging anti-Semitic connotations, can we say that Mary is not only the obedient hand-maiden *(doulē)* of the Lord, but that she is also both faithful and faithless, obedient and interfering, perceptive and opaque, *simul iustus et peccator,* just and sinful alike? Interpreted in this light, Mary not only fulfills a more inclusive typology of Israel in the Old Testament, but she also prefigures the church which is both the spotless Bride of Christ by virtue of God's un-merited grace and, *simul et semper,* the company of pilgrim sinners which must needs pray the Lord's Prayer every day: forgive us our sins.

The Virgin Birth

Evangelicals should be able to affirm without hesitation the Christologi-cal roots of Marian theology as seen in the biblical teaching of Jesus' vir-ginal conception and the patristic affirmation of Mary as God-bearer, Theotokos. I want to examine each of these major Marian motifs in turn.

Subscription to the doctrine of the virgin birth emerged as one of the badges of evangelical orthodoxy during the Fundamentalist-Modernist controversy. J. Gresham Machen, professor at Princeton and later founding president of Westminster Theological Seminary, published in 1930 a major treatise on the virgin birth of Christ. Machen was con-cerned to support the ancient Christian affirmation of the virginal con-ception of Jesus over against the anti-supernaturalistic views set forth at a popular level by Harry Emerson Fosdick and supported in scholarly cir-cles by biblical scholars at the University of Chicago and elsewhere.

Though he was a straight-laced Presbyterian and could never be ac-cused of "cozying up to Rome," Machen rightly recognized that evangeli-cals of his ilk had much more in common with Roman Catholics on this and the other Trinitarian and Christological fundaments of the faith than either of them did with the advocates of what he disdainfully called that, "totally foreign religion — liberalism." "Let it never be forgotten," Machen wrote, "that the virgin birth is an integral part of the New Testa-ment witness about Christ, and that that witness is strongest when it is taken as it stands. . . . The blessed story of the miracle in the virgin's womb is intrinsic to the good news of the Gospel. Only one Jesus is presented in the Word of God; and that Jesus did not come into the world by ordinary generation, but was conceived in the womb of the virgin by the Holy Ghost."[8] Machen did not go so far as some other evangelicals and fundamentalists did in claiming absolutely that no one could be a Christian without believing in the virgin birth. He recognized that the biblical accounts of the virgin birth may not even have been known in some circles of earliest Christianity. But while one might conceivably be a Christian without affirming the virgin birth, there could be no true Christianity among those who denied it.

The virgin birth continued to be a celebrated point of difference between mainline Protestants and their more conservative counterparts during the post–World War II neo-evangelical renaissance. For example, in 1958, *The Christian Century* published an editorial denying the historicity of the virgin birth: the virgin birth, the editorial said, presents Jesus as some kind of tertium quid, half God and half man.[9] Lutheran theologian Arthur Carl Piepkorn commented on this statement: "To account so materially, so biologically, so cellularly for the uniqueness of Jesus is to land dead center on what is precisely *not* the point."[10] This position was consonant with a theological trajectory from Schleiermacher through D. F. Strauss to Paul Tillich, who wrote in the first volume of his *Systematic Theology:* "Apollo has no revelatory significance for Christians; the virgin mother Mary reveals nothing to Protestantism."[11]

To this day, belief in the virgin birth remains a test of true evangelical orthodoxy in that it is one of the few doctrines the denial of which is likely to get one fired in most evangelical schools. However, for all their fervent advocacy of this doctrine, evangelicals may have missed two important aspects of this teaching. In the first place, modern evangelical preoccupation with the virgin birth arose in the context of post-Enlightenment skepticism and reductionism. Evangelicals were concerned to defend the miraculous character of the virgin birth because they saw it undergirding the deity of Jesus Christ. The prominence of the virgin birth teaching among the Apos-

---

8. J. Gresham Machen, *The Virgin Birth of Christ* (Grand Rapids: Baker, 1965; original ed., 1930), pp. 396-97.

9. "A Choice of Miracles," *The Christian Century* 75 (1958): 396.

10. Arthur Carl Piepkorn, "Mary's Place Within the People of God According to Non-Roman Catholics," *Marian Studies* (1967): 51.

11. Paul Tillich, *Systematic Theology* (Chicago: University of Chicago Press, 1951), 1:128.

tolic Fathers and Apologists of the second century, however, arose from a different Christological concern: namely, as an *affirmation of the true humanity and genuine historicity of the Son of God.* "Away with that lowly manger, those dirty swaddling clothes," Marcion had cried.[12] Against all docetism and anti-materialism, Ignatius of Antioch declared in one of the early creedal expressions of the Christian faith that Jesus was "truly born, truly lived, truly *(alethos)* died." That adverb resounds like a gong throughout the writings of the second century: *alethos, alethos, alethos.* This is not to say, of course, that evangelicals are mistaken in their concern about the modernist obscuring and denying of Jesus' true divinity. But in celebrating the virgin birth with the church catholic, we must remember that this teaching is first of all an affirmation of our Lord's humanity.

It is also a fair criticism to note that in their strong defense of the virgin birth, evangelicals have been more concerned with Mary's virginity than with her maternity. Mary was not merely the point of Christ's entrance into the world — the channel through which he passed as water flows through a pipe. She was ever the mother who cared for the physical needs of Jesus the boy. She was the one who nursed him at her breast and who nurtured and taught him the ways of the Lord. Doubtless she was the one who taught him to memorize the Psalms and to pray, even as he grew in wisdom and stature and in favor with God and others (Luke 2:52).

This emphasis on the full humanity of the mother of Jesus is in keeping with the evangelical reticence about the debates over the parturition of Mary. To be sure, there is nothing theologically problematic about affirming Mary's perpetual virginity. This venerable tradition, first given dogmatic sanction at the Fifth Ecumenical Council in 553, was affirmed by Luther, Zwingli, and Calvin during the Reformation, though Calvin was more agnostic about this belief than the other two reformers. Strangely enough, Zwingli attempted to argue for this teaching on the basis of Scripture alone, against the idea that it could only be held on the basis of the teaching authority of the church. His key proof text is Ezekiel 44:2: "This gate is to remain shut. It must not be opened: no one may enter through it. It is to remain shut because the Lord, the God of Israel, has entered through it." When charged with citing this verse out of context,

---

12. On Marcion's docetic Christology, see Jaroslav Pelikan, *The Emergence of the Catholic Tradition* (Chicago: University of Chicago Press, 1971), pp. 71-81.

he replied by quoting 1 Corinthians 10:6: "All these things happened to them by way of example." So much for those who think that the reformers eliminated all allegorical exegesis from their teaching![13]

More problematic than the affirmation of Mary's virginity *postpartum* is the claim for the inviolate virginity of Mary *in partu:* the virgin birth in a precise sense. Not only does this belief stem from a post-canonical writing, the Protoevangelium of James, but it also seems to undermine the anti-docetic emphasis already noted in the emergence of the virgin birth doctrine. This is especially true when it is said that Mary gave birth to Jesus without pain. If indeed the virgin mother of God is the link that unites Christ and humanity, it is hard to see why the virginal conception of Jesus, attested by Scripture, should entail an anesthetized delivery. While Cardinal Newman was surely right to say that God could have spared the mother of the Messiah the pains of child-bearing, there is no sound biblical reason for assuming that God in fact did so. Indeed, if the woman of the Apocalypse in Revelation 12 harks back in any direct way to the real Mary of history, then the opposite seems to be the case, for there we are told that this woman "was pregnant and cried out in pain as she was about to give birth" (Rev. 12:2).

Mary Theotokos

Evangelicals can and should join the church catholic in celebrating the virgin Mary as the mother of God, the God-bearer, or, as Jaroslav Pelikan suggests that we might better render Theotokos, "the one who gave birth to the One who is God."[14] In the Reformation, Calvin (unlike Luther and Zwingli) balked at the title "mother of God" but not at the doctrinal truth it was intended to convey. "To call the virgin Mary the mother of God can only serve to confirm the ignorant in their superstitions," he wrote. "We do not speak of the blood, the head, or the death of God, so neither should we refer to Mary as the mother of God."[15] It may be that

13. David F. Wright, ed., *Chosen by God: Mary in Evangelical Perspective* (London: Marshall Pickering, 1989), p. 171.

14. Jaroslav Pelikan, *Mary Through the Centuries* (New Haven: Yale University Press, 1996), p. 55.

15. Jules Bonnet, ed., *Selected Works of John Calvin: Tracts and Letters* (Grand Rapids: Baker, 1983; original ed., 1858), 5:362.

we see here an indication of Calvin's alleged leaning toward the Nestorian view of Christ.

Both Luther and Calvin sought to remain faithful to the Chalcedonian formula of one person in two natures, though Luther at times leaned toward the Monophysite language, while Calvin leaned in the opposite direction. Barth, however, is faithful to the deepest intention of Reformed Christology when he acknowledges that "mother of God" language for Mary is "sensible, permissible, and necessary as an auxiliary Christological proposition."[16]

Although the conceptual genesis of Theotokos is very early indeed — already Ignatius of Antioch can say "Our God, Jesus Christ, was carried in Mary's womb (Ephesians 18:2)," the debates leading up to the Council of Ephesus were not concerned in the first instance with the status of Mary, but rather with the unity of divinity and humanity in her Son. The church was right to reject Nestorius's preferred title for Mary, "Christotokos," "mother of Christ," as an utterly inadequate description of Mary's role in the mystery of the Incarnation. We are not at liberty to construct a merely human Christ, cut off from the reality of his entire person. Cardinal Ratzinger aptly sums up this important point in the development of doctrine:

> The Christological affirmation of God's Incarnation in Christ becomes necessarily a Marian affirmation, as de facto it was from the beginning. Conversely: only when it touches Mary and becomes Mariology is Christology itself as radical as the faith of the church requires. The appearance of a truly Marian awareness serves as the touchstone indicating whether or not the Christological substance is fully present. Nestorianism involves the fabrication of a Christology from which the nativity and the mother are removed, a Christology without Mariological consequences. Precisely this operation, which surgically removes God so far from man that nativity and maternity — all of corporeality — remain in a different sphere, indicated unambiguously to the Christian consciousness that the discussion no longer concerned incarnation (becoming flesh), that the center of Christ's mystery was endangered, if not already destroyed. Thus in Mariology Christology was defended.[17]

---

16. Karl Barth, *Church Dogmatics* (Edinburgh: T. & T. Clark, 1956), I/2, 138.
17. Ratzinger, *Daughter Zion*, pp. 35-36.

However, there is another dimension of Mary as Theotokos that touches on evangelical sensibilities. Some forty years ago, Heiko A. Oberman published an important article, using the research of Bishop Paulus Rusch of Innsbruck, in which he argued that the negative Nestorian reaction to Theotokos was initially a response to heretical groups who claimed that Mary was the mother of God not only according to the humanity of Christ, but also according to the divinity of Christ, in the same way as there are mothers of gods in pagan religions.[18] Epiphanius of Salamis attested the existence of such heretical groups, one of which he located in Palestine: a community of women who made circular cakes and offered them to the virgin Mary, whom they had come to look upon as a deity. (This group was called the Collyndrians, after the shape of the cakes in their ritual.) Thus, according to Oberman and Rusch, in rightly opposing an exaggerated, heretical Mariolatry, Nestorius himself unwittingly fell into Christological heresy.

While this may be a more charitable reading of Nestorius than the facts warrant, it nonetheless points to a concern registered by Protestant and evangelical critics of subsequent Marian dogmas: Granted the legitimacy of doctrinal development, including the Christological clarification that led to Ephesus and Chalcedon, where are the checks against a Mariological excrescence that so exalts the Virgin that her Son is obscured? Cardinal Newman, of course, put forth seven tests by which the church was to distinguish true development from corruption. Perhaps it goes without saying that to Protestant evangelicals, as well as to Orthodox critics of Roman Catholicism, Cardinal Newman's analysis is least convincing when applied to the most recently declared Marian dogmas of 1854 and 1950.

Handmaiden of the Word

It is regrettable that many evangelicals do not distinguish between official Catholic teaching about Mary and the popular beliefs and practices of Marian devotion. Perhaps the same could be said for many Roman Catholics! Such sensitivity, however, was not lacking among the Fathers of Vatican II. Chapter 8 of *Lumen Gentium* contains a number of statements

18. Heiko A. Oberman, "The Virgin Mary in Evangelical Perspective," *Journal of Ecumenical Studies* 1 (1964): 283.

about Mary which, had they been stated in the sixteenth century with similar clarity, might have prevented the Mariological divide from becoming so deep and wide between the progeny of Rome and the children of the Reformation. For example, the council declares that "it does not wish to decide those questions which the work of theologians has not yet fully clarified." Thus no complete doctrine on Mary is proposed. Likewise, after listing the various titles by which the church refers to Mary — advocate, helper, benefactress, mediatrix — it is stated that none of these "takes away anything from nor adds anything to the dignity or efficacy of Christ the one Mediator. No creature could ever be counted along with the incarnate Word and Redeemer . . . the church does not hesitate to profess this subordinate role of Mary." In addition, while extolling a proper devotion towards Mary, the council strongly urges theologians and preachers "to be careful to refrain as much from all false exaggeration" concerning the special dignity of the mother of God. This is followed by this remarkable sentence: "Let them also carefully refrain from whatever might by word or deed lead the separated brethren or any others whatsoever into error about the true doctrine of the church."[19] In other words, the Blessed Virgin Mary is not to be confused with the most holy and undivided Trinity, but rather is to perform a ministry of unity within the body of Christ. All of this should be encouraging to evangelicals, and other separated brothers (not forgetting the sisters), though there is still much about Mary in *Lumen Gentium* that Reformational Christians cannot embrace.

Insofar as evangelicals are faithful to the heritage of the Reformation, they will listen both to its negative critique of Marian piety and to its positive appraisal of Mary, the handmaiden of the Lord, who heard his word and responded to it in faith. We need not spend much time rehearsing the Mariological developments of the late Middle Ages. Suffice it to say that, following the so-called Anselmian rule, namely, that "one should ascribe to Mary so much purity that more than that one cannot possibly imagine except for God," Mary came to assume more and more an inflated soteriological significance in competition with, and indeed in opposition to, that of Christ himself. Thus, Mary, as *mater misericordia,* ruled the kingdom of mercy while Christ, in the famous pose of Judge on the rainbow, reigned in the kingdom of truth and justice as *iudex*

---

19. *Vatican Council II: The Conciliar and Post-Conciliar Documents,* ed. Austin Flannery (Collegeville, Minn.: Liturgical Press, 1975), pp. 418-23.

vivorum et mortuorum.[20] In this schema, Mary became, as Bernard of Clairvaux put it, "a mediator with the Mediator." Or, as Anselm has it, "She pleads with the Son on behalf of the sons."[21] This led to a view of Mary as co-redemptrix, a term that became popular in the fifteenth century through images of Mary as placating her stern son with milk from her breasts. (This was one reason why Mary's milk, preserved in vials throughout the reliquaries of Europe, were so highly valued. Luther, for example, was shown some of Mary's milk on his famous trip to Rome in 1510.) In this same vein, various texts of Scripture were rewritten with a Marian slant: thus 1 Corinthians 15:22 becomes "as in Eve all die, so also in Mary shall all be made alive." And John 3:16 is rendered: "Mary so loved the world . . . that she gave her only-begotten Son for the salvation of the world." And, anticipating feminist liturgies half a millennium later, the Lord's Prayer began: "Our mother who art in heaven, give us our daily bread."[22]

Luther and all the reformers vehemently protested against the "abominable idolatry" of medieval Mariology. This kind of exaggerated devotion, the reformers held, does not praise the virgin mother of God but in fact slanders her by making her into an idol. Perhaps nowhere is the Protestant reaction to Marian excess more cogently put than in Philipp Melanchthon's "Apology of the Augsburg Confession" of 1530:

> Some of us have seen a certain monastic theologian . . . urge this prayer upon a dying man, "Mother of grace, protect us from the enemy and receive us in the hour of death." Granted that blessed Mary prays for the church, does she receive souls in death, does she overcome death, does she give life? What does Christ do if Mary does all this? . . . The fact of the matter is that in popular estimation the blessed virgin has replaced Christ. People have invoked her, trusted in her mercy, and sought to appease Christ as though He were not a Propitiator but only a terrible Judge and Avenger.[23]

20. Oberman, "Mary in Evangelical Perspective," p. 287.

21. Pelikan, *Mary Through the Centuries,* pp. 125-36. See also Oberman, "Mary in Evangelical Perspective," p. 277.

22. See Richard Bauckham, "The Origins and Growth of Western Mariology," in Wright, *Chosen by God,* pp. 141-60.

23. "Apology for the Augsburg Confession," in T. G. Tappest, ed., *The Book of Concord* (Philadelphia: Fortress Press, 1959), pp. 232-33. Quoted, David F. Wright, "Mary in the Reformers," in Wright, *Chosen by God,* p. 174.

Mary, as Hugh Latimer was to put it, was not to be seen as "a Saviouress."

Yet alongside this critique, there was indeed a positive devotion to Mary among the reformers. Both Zwingli, and Bullinger after him, defended the Ave Maria not as a prayer to Mary, but as an expression of praise in honor of her. Calvin too refers to Mary as "the treasurer of grace," the one who kept faith as a deposit. Through her, Calvin says, we have received this precious gift from God.[24] In 1521, Luther, sequestered in the Wartburg, prepared for press his commentary on the *Magnificat*. Mary is the embodiment of God's unmerited grace. She is magnified above all creatures, and yet it is her humility, lowliness, and indeed noth-ingness *(nichtigkeite)* that is notable. However, Mary is called blessed not because of her virginity or even her humility, "but for this one thing alone, that God regarded her. That is to give all the glory to God as completely as it can be done . . . not she is praised thereby, but God's grace toward her."[25] "I am only the workshop *(fabrica)* in which God operates," Luther has Mary say.[26]

Mary's significance for Luther is twofold. First, Mary is the person and place where God has chosen for his shekinah glory to enter most deeply into the human story. As T. S. Eliot would say, she is "the hint half guessed, the gift half understood . . . the place of impossible union where past and future are conquered and reconciled in incarnation."[27] Second, Mary is also, of course, the one who hears the Word of God — *fides ex auditu,* the one who responds in faith and thus is justified by faith alone. Mary was a disciple before she was a mother, for had she not believed she

---

24. Calvin's *New Testament Commentaries,* ed. David W. Torrance and Thomas F. Torrance (Grand Rapids: Eerdmans, 1972), 1:20-41. This is how Calvin commends a proper reverence for Mary while warning against the excessive devotion of Catholic piety: "She deserves to be called blessed, for God has accorded her a singular distinction, to prepare his Son for the world, in whom she was spiritually reborn. To this day, we cannot enjoy the blessing brought to us in Christ without thinking at the same time of that which God gave us as adornment and honor to Mary, in willing her to be the mother of his only-begotten Son" (32).

25. *LW* 21, 321. See Eric W. Gritsch, "Embodiment of Unmerited Grace: The Virgin Mary According to Martin Luther and Lutheranism," in *Mary's Place in Christian Dialogue,* ed. Alberic Stacpoole (Wilton, Conn.: Morehouse-Barlow, 1982), pp. 133-41.

26. *WA* 7, 573: *"Ego nihil sum quam fabrica, in qua Deus operatur . . ."* Quoted in Oberman, "Mary in Evangelical Perspective," p. 288.

27. T. S. Eliot, "Four Quartets," in *The Complete Poems and Plays, 1909-1950* (New York: Harcourt, Brace and World, 1971), p. 136.

would not have conceived. And this faith too is not the achievement of merit, but the gift of grace. Mary is the object of God's gracious predestination, and this divine choice is the source of both her blessedness and her fertility. At this point, Barth is the preeminent evangelical theologian who is fully in line with the Reformation message when he declares (against Bultmann) that redemption is wrought by Christ "outside of us, without us, and even against us." This means that when we praise and love Mary, it is God whom we praise for his gracious favor to his chosen handmaid.

As the embodiment of *sola gratia* and *sola fide,* that is, the material and formal principles of the Reformation, Mary should be thus highly extolled in evangelical theology and worship. Why is this not the case? Why do evangelicals remember the Reformation critique of Marian excess but not the positive appraisal of Mary's indispensable role in God's salvific work?

Doubtless there are many answers to this question, but I would like to mention just two. The first is the pruning effect of the scriptural principle itself. Luther closed his commentary on the Magnificat in 1521 with a prayer of intercession addressed to the virgin Mary. But already in Zwingli's *Sixty-seven Articles* of 1523, it was claimed that because Christ is our only Mediator, no mediators other than Christ are needed beyond this life. Luther too gave up Marian intercession when he could find no explicit scriptural warrant for it in the Bible. (As a Baptist, I might be forgiven for noting Luther's inconsistency in retaining infant baptism, which also has no explicit biblical warrant!) In the next century George Herbert addressed a poem to Mary in which he explains the lack of Protestant petitions to her:

> Not out of envie or maliciousnesse
> Do I forbear to crave your speciall aid;
>   I would address
> My vows to thee most gladly, blessed Maid,
> And Mother of my God, in my distresse.
>
> Thou art the holy mine, whence came the gold,
> The great restorative for all decay
>   In young and old;

Thou art the cabinet where the jewell lay:
Chiefly to thee I would my soul unfold.

But now (alas!) I dare not; for our King,
Whom we all joyntly do adore and praise,
    Bids no such thing:
And where his pleasure no injunction layes,
('Tis your own case) ye never move a wing.

All worship is prerogative, and a flower
Of his rich crown, from whom lyes no appeal
    At the last houre:
Therefore we dare not from his garland steal,
To make a posie for inferiour power.

Although then others court you, if ye know
What's done on earth, we shall not fare the worse,
    Who do not so;
Since we are ever ready to disburse,
If any one our Master's hand can show.[28]

Beyond the theological constraints of a religion of the Book, however, there was also within the Protestant and evangelical traditions what might be called an ecclesiological hardening of the arteries. To be an evangelical meant *not* to be a Roman Catholic. To worship Jesus meant *not* to honor Mary, even if such honor were biblically grounded and liturgically chaste.

In some quarters of the evangelical world the loss of catholicity was marked by a disdain for creedal Christianity. Thus in 1742 when the Philadelphia Baptist Association published a confession of faith and commended it to the churches for their approval, the Baptists who wanted "no creed but the Bible" could think of nothing nastier to say about the Philadelphia Confession than to call it a new virgin Mary. "We need no such virgin Mary to come between us and God," they said. In time, of course, some evangelicals not only threw the virgin Mary overboard, they also abandoned the Holy Trinity. This was especially true in England,

28. George Herbert, "To All Angels and Saints," in *The Complete English Poems,* ed. John Tobin (London: Penguin, 1991), pp. 71-72.

where virtually the entire denomination of General or Arminian Baptists converted en masse to Unitarianism.[29]

In the context of this development, it is nothing less than astounding to come across a remarkable book published in 1886 by A. Stewart Walsh and introduced by the popular evangelical preacher, T. DeWitt Talmage. The book is entitled *Mary: The Queen of the House of David and Mother of Jesus.* A magnum opus of 626 pages, it reads somewhat like an extensive Harlequin romance of Mary's life, highly romanticized and fictionalized, a paean of praise to motherhood in general of which Mary of course is the chief exemplar. However, near the end of this fanciful tome, there is this plea for a proper evangelical recognition of Mary:

> But this only, and surely, here I know, no friend of the divine Son can dethrone Him by honoring her, aright; indeed, as He, Himself did. It was of Him she spoke when exclaiming: "My soul doth rejoice in God my Savior!" Can one truly honor Him and despise and ignore the woman who gave Him human birth? Can one have His mind and forget her for whom love was uppermost to Him in His supreme last hours? Can one honor her aright, and yet dethrone the Son whom she enthroned when she bore Him, then lived for Him? She honored herself in bearing Him, and was His mother, His teacher and His disciple. He revered her, she worshiped Him.[30]

Mother of the Church

Even before Vatican II, Father Georges Florovsky had observed that Mariology should not be a separate treatise in theology but rather a chapter in a treatise on the Incarnation. At Vatican II there was heated debate on whether to develop a separate document on Mary, but by a close vote the decision was made to treat Mary in the context of ecclesiology. Is there a sense in which evangelicals too can speak of Mary as *mater ecclesiae?* I think there is, although not with the same nuances imputed to this term by Roman Catholic ecclesiology. Vatican II speaks of the pil-

29. See Raymond Brown, *The English Baptists of the Eighteenth Century* (London: Baptist Historical Society, 1986).

30. A. Stewart Walsh, *Mary: The Queen of the House of David and Mother of Jesus* (New York: Henry S. Allen, 1886), p. 555.

grim church that "presses forward amid the persecutions of the world and the consolations of God" (*LG,* 8). The New Testament portrays Mary as among the last at the cross, and the first in the Upper Room. She is thus a bridging figure not only between the Old and New Testaments at Jesus' birth, but also between the close of his earthly ministry and the outpouring of the Holy Spirit in the Pentecostal birthday of the church. It is significant that in Eastern iconography, Mary is never depicted alone, but always with Christ, the apostles, and the saints.

It is particularly Mary at the foot of the cross, *sous la croix,* that speaks to the ecclesial reality of the church as a faithful remnant. Already before the Reformation, the idea of the remnant church emerged as a major motif in late medieval ecclesiology. The Blessed Virgin Mary was seen as the archetype of the remnant church: her faithfulness alone kept the catholic church intact during Christ's passion on the cross. When all of the disciples (including Peter!) had fled in fear, Mary remained true to Christ and his word. Her fidelity under the cross showed that the true faith could be preserved in one sole individual, and thus Mary became the mother of the (true remnant) church. As we have seen, the reformers honored Mary and even defended the use of the Ave Maria, because they were so impressed by Mary's submission to the Word of God and her fidelity to it *contra mundum.*

The other scriptural text in which Mary emerges as the mother of the church is the apocalyptic vision of Revelation 12. Here the woman who gives birth to a son is harassed and pursued by the dragon. This recalls Luther's lyrical hymn of 1525 praising the church:

To me she is dear, the worthy maid, and I cannot forget her;
Praise, honor, virtue of her are said; then all I love her better.

On earth, all mad with murder, the mother now alone is she,
But God will watchful guard her, and the right Father be.[31]

To the eyes of faith the church is a "worthy maid," the Bride of Christ, but by the standards of the world she is a poor Cinderella surrounded by many dangerous foes.

If, then, a person desires to draw the church as he sees her, he will picture her as a deformed and poor girl sitting in an unsafe forest in the

31. *LW* 53, 293.

midst of hungry lions, bears, wolves, and boars, nay, deadly serpents; in the midst of infuriated men who set sword, fire, and water in motion in order to kill her and wipe her from the face of the earth.[32]

In God's sight the church is pure, holy, unspotted, the Dove of God; but in the eyes of the world, it bears the form of a servant. It is like its Bridegroom, Christ: "hacked to pieces, marked with scratches, despised, crucified, mocked" (Isa. 53:2-3).[33]

Mary *sous la croix* speaks to the pilgrim church, which is also increasingly the persecuted church. Precisely as the woman pursued by the dragon, Mary stands in solidarity with her Orthodox, Catholic, and evangelical children who also live under the shadow of the cross and whose faithful witness is even now leading many of them to the shedding of their blood. Thus in *Ut Unum Sint*, Pope John Paul II calls us all to remember the courageous witness of so many martyrs of our century, including members of "churches and ecclesial communities not in full communion with the Catholic Church."

Conclusion

Baptist preachers always have three points and a poem; I have given you five points and now two poems. Both poems in a sense are commentaries on the famous painting by Matthias Grünewald from the Isenheim Altarpiece, which shows John the Baptist pointing with his long bony finger to Christ writhing in the agonies of death on the cross. In faded red letters, in Latin, are the words: "He must increase, I must decrease." A copy of this painting hung over the desk of Karl Barth in Basel where it still remains today. It was Barth's contention that the figure of John pointing, not to himself nor to anyone else, but to Christ alone *(solus christus)* was the perfect prototype for all preachers and theologians whose vocation should be governed by the Johannine text: "Behold, the Lamb of God who takes away the sin of the world" (John 1:29). What is often not recognized is that the Blessed Virgin Mary is also a prominent figure in this painting. She too stands under the cross, not, as usual, with John the Be-

---

32. *WA* 40/3, 315.
33. *LW* 54, 262.

loved Disciple but here with John the Baptist. Here she represents the church in its primary vocation and call to discipleship.

This is a Mary whom evangelicals can and should embrace. We do not think of the mother of God in isolation from her Son, an object of devotion by herself. Rather, as the Anglican poet-chaplain of World War I, G. A. Studdert Kennedy, expressed it in a poem titled "Good Friday Falls on Lady Day,"

> And has our Lady lost her place?
> Does her white star burn dim?
> Nay, she has lowly veiled her face
> Because of Him.
>
> Men give to her the jewelled crown,
> And robe with broidered rim,
> But she is fain to cast them down
> Because of Him.
>
> She claims no crown from Christ apart,
> Who gave God life and limb,
> She only claims a broken heart
> Because of Him.[34]

The final poem is by a Baptist Welsh New Testament scholar named John Gwili Jenkins. The poem is titled "Wales and the Virgin Mary."

> Greetings, blessed mother of Jesus
> Heaven and earth's *Ave* be to you.
> Let me after mute ages return
> Before you to offer belated praise to your fame.
>
> There were days in Wales when the praise
> Of my Lord's mother was on every pure tongue;
> From every valley arose incense
> On every mountain your hill of anguish was recalled.
>
> Now, the happy chatting is finished in the many
> Porches of churches that were places of holiness;

---

34. G. A. Studdert Kennedy, *The Unutterable Beauty* (London: Hodder and Stoughton, 1947), p. 98.

And no longer do we hear the sweet smell of incense
From the many altars of your intercession.

Forgive us, gentle maiden, if we learnt to give you
Less respect than heaven would have wished;
For we fell in love with the Son of your great love,
So as not to venerate you more than Him.

Teach us, blessed virgin, once more to pay our fathers'
    debt of praise;
And when Christendom calls you blessed
Let no spot in blessed Wales be mute.[35]

Thanks be to God!

35. The papers of John Gwili Jenkins (1872-1936) are in the National Library of Wales. This poem is discussed in A. M. Allchin, *The Joy of All Creation: An Anglican Meditation on the Place of Mary* (Cambridge, Mass.: Cowley, 1984).

Contributors

Carl E. Braaten, Executive Director, Center for Catholic and Evangelical Theology; Co-Editor, *Pro Ecclesia*

Lawrence S. Cunningham, John A. O'Brien Professor of Theology, Notre Dame University, Notre Dame, Indiana

Kyriaki Karidoyanes FitzGerald, Orthodox Theologian and Psychologist, Sagamore, Massachusetts

Beverly Roberts Gaventa, Helen H. P. Manson Professor of New Testament Literature and Exegesis, Princeton Seminary, Princeton, New Jersey

Timothy George, Dean, Beeson Divinity School, Samford University, Birmingham, Alabama

Robert W. Jenson, Senior Scholar for Research, Center of Theological Inquiry, Princeton, New Jersey; Co-Editor, *Pro Ecclesia*

Jaroslav Pelikan, Sterling Professor of History Emeritus, Yale University, New Haven, Connecticut

David S. Yeago, Michael C. Peeler Professor of Systematic Theology, Lutheran Theological Southern Seminary, Columbia, South Carolina